Praise

"I feel in my heart that I finally have some parameters and guidance to the path of healing. I want to thank you in advance from the bottom of my heart that I'm so happy God put you on this earth to help others despite your own pain and suffering. God Bless You always!"

—Angel W.

"Very intrigued by vibrational energy and loved, loved, loved the part of 'what if' when encountering resistance, which I do. I will absolutely be using that. This is just what I needed. It feels like nurturing to me, cozy and positive, a break from my hectic schedule."

—Laura M.

"This book is an amazing guide for anyone who has been affected (infected) by a toxic relationship with a narcissistic relative (sibling, partner, parent, etc.!!) Diane Metcalf skillfully outlines so many great strategies for changing one's negative, destructive thought patterns to positive, empowering affirmations! It really is a must-read and "must share!""

—Patti E.

Lemon Moms:

Life-Altering Affirmations

Change Your Self-talk, Change YourSELF

Diane Metcalf

Copyright © 2021 Image and Aspect Media
Lemon Moms: Life-Altering Affirmation, Change Your Self-talk, Change YourSELF

All rights reserved. No part of this publication may be reproduced, distributed or transmitted in any form or by any means, including photocopying, recording, or other electronic or mechanical methods, without the prior written permission of the publisher, except in the case of brief quotations embodied in critical reviews and certain other noncommercial uses permitted by copyright law.

Although the author and publisher have made every effort to ensure that the information in this book was correct at press time, the author and publisher do not assume and hereby disclaim any liability to any party for any loss, damage, or disruption caused by errors or omissions, whether such errors or omissions result from negligence, accident, or any other cause. Adherence to all applicable laws and regulations, including international, federal, state and local governing professional licensing, business practices, advertising, and all other aspects of doing business in the US, Canada or any other jurisdiction is the sole responsibility of the reader and consumer.

Neither the author nor the publisher assumes any responsibility or liability whatsoever on behalf of the consumer or reader of this material. Any perceived slight of any individual or organization is purely unintentional.

The resources in this book are provided for informational purposes only. They should not be used to replace the specialized training and professional judgment of a health care or mental health care professional.

Neither author nor publisher can be held responsible for the use of the information provided within this book. Please always consult a trained professional before making any decision regarding treatment of yourself or others.

For more information, email Diane@DianeMetcalf.com

Cover design by Diane Metcalf
ISBN 978-1-7352876-4-5

FREE GIFT

To get the best experience from this book, please download my beautiful, soothing phone-screen affirmations wallpaper.

Be reminded of your affirmational goals whenever you look at your phone!

Download here:

toolbox.dianemetcalf.com/freeaffirmations

I appreciate you!

DEDICATION

*For the invisible and scapegoat children.
Be seen. Be heard.*

Contents

FOREWORD 15
PREFACE 19
INTRODUCTION 25
Chapter One WHY USE AFFIRMATIONS? 29
How Affirmations Work 30
A Positive Mindset 30
Affirmation Theory 31
The Research 32
Self-Perspectives and Other Beliefs 34
Chapter Two HEALING AFFIRMATIONS 36
Negative and Unsupportive 36
Doing the Work 37
Chapter Three HOW TO BEGIN 40
Affirmations and the Law of Attraction 41
Let's Get High 44
Mindfulness 45
Thoughts Become Things 46
Short, Clear, Concrete, Positive and Present Tense 47
How Many? 53
Safe and Accessible 55
Recap 56
Chapter Four FOUR FUNDAMENTALS 57
Intend 58
Affirm 59
Ask 61
Gratitude, Gratitude, Gratitude 62
Chapter Five WHO YOU ARE, REALLY 64
Your Authentic Self 64
Positive Affirmations vs. Codependency 65
Chapter Six DEALING WITH TOXIC PEOPLE ... 66

The Dilemma *66*
Affirmations to Counteract Negativity *69*
My Healing Affirmations *75*
Chapter Seven STAND IN YOUR POWER 76
Covert Narcissistic Mothers *76*
Affirmations For Standing in Your Power *79*
My Healing Affirmations *86*
Chapter Eight HEALING THE FIGHT OR FLIGHT RESPONSE 87
Remembering the Past *87*
Emotional Regulation *88*
Affirmations For Calming Fight or Flight *89*
My Healing Affirmations *95*
Chapter Nine FEELING VALIDATED 96
Not Good Enough Codependents *96*
Invisible and Silent *97*
On Being Seen and Heard *97*
Talking With Your Mother *99*
The Fantasy *99*
Affirmations for Self-validation *101*
My Healing Affirmations *109*
Chapter Ten WORKING THROUGH NARCISSISM AWARENESS 110
A Special Kind of Grief *110*
Awakening *111*
Affirmations for Working Through Narcissism Awareness Grief *114*
My Healing Affirmations *119*
Chapter Eleven HEALING BLAME AND REJECTION 120
Projection and Scapegoating *121*
Affirmations to Feel Accepted *123*
My Healing Affirmations *130*

Chapter Twelve HEALING BETRAYAL WOUNDS 131
Narcissistic Lies..............131
Affirmations to Heal Betrayal Wounds..............134
My Healing Affirmations 140
Chapter Thirteen HEALING EMOTIONAL ABANDONMENT 141
Punitive Silence..............141
Affirmations to Feel Safe..............144
My Healing Affirmations 150
Chapter Fourteen HEALING SHAME 151
What Shame Feels Like..............151
Affirmations to Heal Shame..............154
My Healing Affirmations 161
Chapter Fifteen EMOTIONALLY DETACHING . 162
Narcissistic Supply..............162
Denying the Supply..............163
Affirmations to Set and Maintain Healthy Boundaries..............165
My Healing Affirmations 171
Chapter Sixteen OVERCOMING THREATS AND RAGES 172
Uncontrolled Outrage..............172
Affirmations to Feel Secure..............174
My Healing Affirmations 180
Chapter Seventeen HEALING FROM GASLIGHTING 181
Seeds of Doubt..............181
Self-gaslighting..............182
Affirmations for Improving Self-trust..............184
My Healing Affirmations 191
Chapter Eighteen HEALING CODEPENDENCY 192
How Codependency Develops..............193

Affirmations to Heal Codependency......*195*
My Healing Affirmations *201*
Chapter Nineteen HEALING PTSD and C-PTSD. 202
PTSD vs. C-PTSD *202*
Triggering......*203*
Affirmations to Heal C-PTSD Triggers *205*
My Healing Affirmations *211*
Chapter Twenty A NEW BEGINNING 212
Indicators of Recovery *213*
Glossary of Terms...... 223
References 231
Bibliography 237
Enhance Your Experience 239
Acknowledgments 241
About the Author 243
What's Next? 245
Love This Book? 247

Your thoughts and beliefs of the past have created this moment and all the moments up to this moment. What you are now choosing to believe and think and say will create the next moment and the next day and the next month and the next year.

You have the power to heal your life, and you need to know that. We think so often that we are helpless, but we're not. We always have the power of our minds...Claim and consciously use your power.

*"I change my life when I change my thinking.
I am Light. I am Spirit.
I am a wonderful, capable being.
And it is time for me to acknowledge
that I create my own reality with my thoughts.
If I want to change my reality,
then it is time for me to change my mind."*

-Louise Hay

FOREWORD

I met Diane through a mutual friend, and I connected with her the moment we began talking. We quickly became friends and would talk often.

In our discussions, we shared our stories, our different career paths, and we found many commonalities, and that we both had experienced childhood with a self-absorbed parent. She has a narcissistic mother, and both of my parents were narcissistic. Yep, that is right. Life growing up was a bit confusing. I explain to people I grew up in La La Land and entering into the real world was a tough transition, with years of searching to understand why life seemed so upside down.

We connected in our journeys to healing.

Diane's dedication to becoming whole again, and to help other people do the same, is inspiring. She has left no stone unturned by taking the time to research, apply, and review the available healing tools, including the old and new science. She has the experience, the intelligence, the intuition, and the results to speak on the topic of healing from narcissistic abuse.

I believe it is important to understand the "theory" behind each concept of healing and the fact that words DO matter. In this book filled with positive affirmation theory, she has eloquently and concisely delivered this powerful process. She will help you understand and apply these Life- Altering Affirmations. This book is simply an excellent tool for healing, growth, and fulfillment in your life.

As a Massage Therapist of sixteen years, and an Alternative Wellness Practitioner of ten years, I found that when I taught my clients the physiology or the psychology of the therapy and the therapeutic benefits of the modality, their mindset would change to allow the treatment to be received for the most benefit possible.

Diane teaches with such a high level of healing science, alongside the rare vibrational and energetic component of healing. Her compilations of affirmations are extensive, and she groups them to address the specific abuse patterns the reader needs. The ability to be able to use these immediately makes them even more empowering.

I am excited for you to transform your life and as you understand, embrace, and apply this powerful healing process with Diane's life-changing book.

Ellen MaRee

PREFACE

WORDS MATTER

If you've read "Lemon Moms: A Guide to Understand and Survive Maternal Narcissism," you know that my mother used the fear of abandonment to manipulate and control me as a child. She threatened to give me away, put me in an orphanage, or send me to live with my father, whom she repeatedly said: "didn't love us or want anything to do with us."

I lived in constant fear of doing the "right thing," whatever the right thing was at any particular time. "The right thing" could and did change without warning, so I needed to remain constantly alert for changes in her tone of voice, behavior, and our home environment.

My mom parented by blaming, shaming, intimidating, threatening, and physically punishing. In the earliest years of my life, I learned that I was somehow to blame for everything that displeased her. Second-guessing and doubting myself became my way of life. I felt like a burden, believing that I made her life harder simply because I existed. I stayed out of her way as much as possible. I felt lonely and alone.

Mother shared thoughts and feelings with me in frightening, highly emotionally charged, biased, and inappropriate ways. Gaslighting and the resulting cognitive dissonance distorted my perceptions and beliefs. My codependency had begun. Her behavior initiated the codependency process, but her words guaranteed it.

THE POWER OF WORDS

Words matter. Written words, spoken words, they all matter. It matters what people say to you, and it matters what you say to yourself. For example, suppose you live with a narcissist or toxic person (or have one in your life). In that case, you already know that it can negatively affect how you think about yourself, what you tell yourself, and how you treat yourself.

Oblivious of my codependency, her words and my negative self-talk combined to confirm my beliefs; I was unlovable, would never be good enough, and didn't matter.

The combination of the negative self-talk and the limiting beliefs kept me in a state of learned helplessness. Eventually, as an adult, I woke up to the fact that I was stuck. I'd been repeating the same hurtful relationship patterns throughout my adult life and wondering why I was unhappy. Finally, I realized that something had to change. So, among other things, I started examining, questioning and then changing my unsupportive inner dialogue into supportive, positive self-talk. I watched in amazement as my limiting beliefs began to fade away. As I started thinking differently about myself, my self-concept changed. My opinions about myself changed. *I* changed.

How's YOUR Self-talk?

Have you ever *really* observed how you talk to yourself? Some of us are not very nice to ourselves, and others are just plain abusive. What kinds of things do you say to yourself? Is your self-talk positive and loving? Or maybe you beat yourself up and tell yourself hurtful things?

Have you ever tried talking to yourself as you would speak with a friend? How would that feel? Try being understanding, considerate, and kind to yourself. You would do that for your friend, right? You would encourage her, or him or them, wouldn't you? You can start doing the same for yourself right now. Acknowledging your feelings about yourself when you make a mistake or struggle and choosing to comfort and care for yourself is called "self-compassion." Self-compassion promotes positive, healthy self-care practices and a healthy mindset, which help to heal codependency.

It's not surprising to know that what we tell ourselves is linked to how we feel about ourselves. Changing your self-talk from an unsupportive inner dialogue to an uplifting and proactive one brings about positive change. But, if you beat yourself up for perceived failures or shortcomings, how does that help you? Does it motivate you to change? Does it keep you feeling bad and keep you stuck? How is it different from how your narcissistic mother treated you?

Do you tell yourself, "I'm just _____," or "I've just always been this way," or "that's just how I've always been"? I have a couple of things to say about these types of comments: first, stop using the word "just." When you add "just," it implies that what you're saying has low significance. It sounds apologetic and meek. Don't believe me? Take the word "just" out of your self-talk. Say it with and without the word "just." Do you see how it feels different? Are you more confident? Empowered? Serious? You tell me.

And what we say to ourselves isn't only a description of what we believe about ourselves; it is a *command*. Your self-talk TELLS your mind what to think about you! When you tell yourself, "this is just who I am," "I've always been _____," or "I've always done _____," it implies that there's no room for change. These statements tell your brain, "this is it. This is final. There is no more." Why would you want to do that? Chances are, you don't know you're doing it, and this is where self-awareness comes in. Start becoming aware of how you speak to yourself and the words that you use. Notice and take note for future reference.

Now, give yourself a break. You're a human being, and no human being has ever been or will ever be perfect. Perfection doesn't exist. Instead of comparing yourself to a non-existent standard, try focusing on your progress.

Results happen over time. Making positive life change is about ***progress, not perfection.*** Encourage yourself the way you'd encourage your friend or a small child. Tell yourself, "You've got this!" and eventually, you will get it! Be patient with yourself. It takes time to learn new things. Treating yourself with kindness, patience, and compassion does a lot towards reparenting yourself and healing your inner child too.

ACTION TIME

Thinking about and remembering what happened in our childhoods doesn't promote healing. That's where many of us get stuck. Recovery requires more than reading, educating ourselves, and revisiting old memories. It requires action: getting in touch with our feelings, prioritizing self-care, dumping limiting beliefs, learning to set boundaries and enforce them, learning new ways of communicating, increasing self-esteem and self-confidence, doing inner child and reparenting work, and emotionally detaching.

It means doing the *work,* and I believe it begins with changing our unconscious, negative self-talk.

INTRODUCTION

Until I began my healing journey in earnest, I continued to attract toxic people and exercise my codependency. I fixed and helped others without their invitation to do so. I felt resentful when they ignored my advice or were unappreciative of my help. It makes no sense, right? It didn't feel great either.

Reading, researching, and working through assorted therapies eventually led me into Narcissism Awareness Grief. Once there, I finally came to terms with my childhood experiences and learned how, unhealed, they affected my adult relationships. I worked through the stages and continued learning coping skills like setting boundaries, emotionally detaching, improving self-care, and practicing strategic communication. As I found my voice and spoke my truth, my confidence and self-esteem grew. I began feeling whole and worthy for the first time in my life.

Narcissism specialists say that we have two choices when dealing with narcissists and those on the narcissistic spectrum: live on their terms or go "no contact." I suggest we have a third option: walk through the chaos and confusion armed with new coping skills, protected by boundaries, speaking our truth, and enjoying life as our true selves. I hope you find the path that works for you.

Diane

LEMON MOMS:
LIFE-ALTERING AFFIRMATIONS

Chapter One
WHY USE AFFIRMATIONS?

I talk about codependency a lot in *Lemon Moms: A Guide to Understand and Survive Maternal Narcissism*. Codependency is at the very core of the changes we must make to heal from any kind of mistreatment or abuse.

Codependency is described as a set of maladaptive coping skills. They are typically learned in childhood due to feeling unsafe in the home environment. Living with real or perceived threats made it necessary for those who grew up like this to monitor our settings and control people and outcomes as best we could. It eventually felt natural to do this, and it became a way of life. Codependency can also be learned by imitating other codependents. It can be passed down through generations. This is known as "generational trauma."

If we're codependent, we grew up to be "people-pleasers." We willingly play by the rules of others, losing our identity in the process. We rely on others for a sense of identity, approval, or affirmation. We support and "enable" others in their addictions, mental illness, immaturity, irresponsibility, or under-achievement.

When we're bogged down in codependency, it's impossible to know our true, authentic selves. By using affirmations, we can become aware of our codependent thoughts and behavior and replace them with healthy, functional ones. We can finally connect with our authentic selves.

How Affirmations Work

Connecting with our authentic selves requires doing the necessary work to uncover our true selves for the first time. We can do this with affirmations.

Affirmations remind us of who we are when we are our authentic selves. By following our intuition, writing, and speaking positive affirmations, we can begin honoring and eventually becoming our true selves. Affirmations help us to find ourselves and create our best lives possible.

A Positive Mindset

Affirmations are designed to promote an optimistic mindset; they have been shown to reduce the tendency to dwell on negative experiences (Wiesenfeld et al., 2001.) Optimism is a powerful perception! When we replace negative thoughts with positive ones, we are creating a whole new narrative around "who we are" and what we can accomplish.

AFFIRMATION THEORY

There are three fundamental ideas involved in self-affirmation theory. Correctly written affirmations work according to this theory:

1. By using positive affirmations, we can change our self-identity. Affirmations reinforce a newly created self-narrative; we become flexible and capable of adapting to different conditions (Cohen & Sherman, 2014.) Now, instead of viewing ourselves in a fixed or rigid way (for example, as "lazy"), we are flexible in our thoughts. We can adopt a broader range of "identities" and roles and define things like "success" differently. We can view various aspects of ourselves as positive and adapt to different situations more easily (Aronson, 1969.)

2. Self-identity is not about being exceptional, perfect, or excellent (Cohen & Sherman, 2014). Instead, we need to be competent and adequate in areas that we value (Steele, 1988.)

3. We maintain self-integrity by behaving in ways that genuinely deserve acknowledgment and praise. We

say an affirmation because we want to integrate that particular personal value into our own identity.

THE RESEARCH

Claude Steele, a social psychologist and emeritus professor at Stanford University, promoted self-affirmation theory in the late 1980s (Steele, C. M. 1988, Cohen, G. L., & Sherman, D. K. 2007).

Affirmation research focuses on how individuals adapt to information or experiences that threaten their self-image. Today, self-affirmation theory remains well-studied throughout social psychological research (Sherman, D. K., & Cohen, G. L., McQueen, A., & Klein, W. M. (2006.)

Self-affirmation theory has led to research in neuroscience and investigating whether we can "see" how the brain changes using imaging technology while using positive affirmations. MRI evidence suggests that specific neural pathways increase when we speak affirmations (Cascio et al., 2016). The "ventromedial prefrontal cortex," involved in positive self-evaluation and self-related information processing, becomes more active when we speak positively about our values (Falk et al., 2015; Cascio et al., 2016).

Dr. Emily Falk and her colleagues focused on how people process information about themselves. They discovered that by using positive affirmations, "otherwise-threatening information" is seen as more self-relevant and valuable (2015: 1979). Cohen and Sherman found that using self-affirmations can help with threats or stress and that they can be beneficial for improving academic performance, health, and wellbeing (Cohen, G. L., & Sherman, D. K. 2014).

And Dr. Peter Harris' research found that when using affirmations, smokers responded less dismissively to cigarette packet warnings and conveyed the intention to change their behavior (Harris et al., 2007).

The evidence suggests that affirmations are beneficial in multiple ways!

Positive affirmations:

1. have been shown to decrease health-related stress (Sherman et al., 2009; Critcher & Dunning, 2015.)

2. have been used effectively in "Positive Psychology Interventions," or PPI, scientific tools and strategies used for increasing happiness, well-being, positive thinking, and emotions (Keyes, Fredrickson, & Park, 2012.)

3. may help change the perception of otherwise "threatening" messages (Logel & Cohen, 2012.)

4. can help us set our intention to change for the better (Harris et al., 2007) (Epton & Harris, 2008.)

5. have been positively linked to academic achievement by lessening GPA decline in students who felt isolated in college (Layous et al., 2017.)

6. have been demonstrated to lower stress (Koole et al., 1999; Weisenfeld et al., 2001.)

7. provide health benefits by helping us respond in a less defensive or resistant manner when we perceive threats.

In a nutshell, using affirmations allows us to create an adaptive, broader self-concept, making us more resilient to life's struggles. Whether it's social pressure, health, or healing trauma, a broader self-concept is a valuable tool.

SELF-PERSPECTIVES AND OTHER BELIEFS

Louise Hay was an American author, teacher, and motivational speaker who survived several difficult and traumatic experiences, including domestic violence and cancer.

After being diagnosed with terminal cancer in the 1970s, she began searching for a non-medical healing alternative. She created a new healing approach combining visualization, forgiveness, psychotherapy, and nutritional cleansing using what she learned.

Hay argued that negative beliefs could cause health problems. She understood that we could transform our lives and health by using healing affirmations. She believed her new healing approach cured her cervical cancer within six months of diagnosis.

She published **Heal Your Body** in 1976, long before the mind-body connection was a household concept. Her international bestseller **You Can Heal Your Life** was published in 1984.

Hay is considered a founder of the self-help movement and lived to the age of ninety. Because of her, millions have come to understand the power of using healing affirmations to develop thought patterns that reverse illness, and now you can too!

Chapter Two
HEALING AFFIRMATIONS

Simply stated, a healing affirmation is a positive statement about your physical or emotional wellbeing. Healing affirmations are based on the belief that your thoughts influence your physical and emotional health. The great thing is you don't have to be sick to use healing affirmations!

NEGATIVE AND UNSUPPORTIVE

You might be more familiar with negative affirmations, the hurtful, unkind, and destructive things we tell ourselves. They are the unsupportive inner dialogue that runs in the background of our thoughts. We hear them as that little voice that whispers, "you're too fat to be wearing that," or "none of these people care about what you think," or "you're not smart enough to do that." Those negative affirmations can do a lot of harm to our self-confidence and self-esteem. It's time to replace them with *positive* affirmations! Let's kick negativity out of our lives altogether. We're on a healing journey, and negative self-talk has no place in our lives anymore.

If we grew up in dysfunction, especially in a narcissistic home, we understood that we couldn't do anything right and that we weren't good enough or didn't matter. Whether intentional or not, if we had a narcissistic mother, her words and behavior, like emotional knives, cut us deeply. And long after we left home, that cruel, critical, internalized voice stayed with us.

We may try convincing ourselves that we're over-reacting, that she didn't mean any harm, or that it never really happened (self-gaslighting.) Denying the reality of our childhood and allowing emotional wounds to remain unaddressed and unhealed leaves us unprepared to face life's challenges as adults. Our unhealed triggers and wounded inner child can keep us stuck perceiving, feeling, and responding like a frightened child.

Doing the Work

When we've done the work and progressed through the stages of Narcissism Awareness Grief, a term coined by Dr. Christine Hammond, to arrive at the final phase of acceptance, it may feel as though a huge burden has been lifted. We are finally able to fully confront the reality of our past. It is as if a blindfold was removed; we can see our history and how it relates to who we are *now* and who *we can be in the future*. We're not fearful or threatened by this understanding. We have a new sense of the "bigger picture." All of the bits and pieces combine to give us a fresh new perspective and experience of ourselves and an awareness of our personal power. We feel hope. We feel grateful for allowing ourselves to question our past: in doing the work, we question the things we've been told were true, and we challenge those unsupportive inner voices.

We no longer feel the need to push our feelings or memories away. Now, we can sit with them and observe. And as we watch, we see our story unfold. We write, or talk, about it. We acknowledge the courageous little children we were, faced with childhoods full of confusion, doubt, and shame, and we feel compassion for ourselves. We finally know what we want from ourselves and our lives, and we're willing to start making the necessary changes to get it. We know we'll be OK. We know we've got this.

Working through Narcissism Awareness Grief is discussed at length in chapter ten. Using strong healing affirmations will help in each stage of Narcissism Awareness Grief, and in living beyond "Acceptance." They can help with boundary setting, feeling safe, improving self-trust and self-esteem, increasing self-confidence and personal empowerment, and healing C-PTSD symptoms. When we are suffering from C-PTSD, our minds attempt to ensure our safety by alerting us to stored memories of similar feeling threats. If we avoid these painful memories by actively denying, disconnecting from, and rejecting them, the trauma *remains unaddressed and unhealed*. C-PTSD is discussed at length in chapter nineteen.

The affirmations in this book may be used as they are. Still, I invite you to personalize them and make them your own as you learn to write your own effective healing affirmations.

Let's get started!

Chapter Three
HOW TO BEGIN

The "Law of Attraction" is a viewpoint that suggests thinking positive thoughts can bring about positive effects, and holding negative thoughts can bring adverse outcomes. This law is based on the belief that thoughts are a form of energy, so positive thoughts attract positive energy and vice versa.

Human beings are energy fields, and every human body is made of energy-producing particles in constant motion. So, everything in existence, including us humans, vibrates at particular frequencies and creates energy. (Srinivasan 2010.)

There's growing evidence that our body's own electrical and magnetic energy can stimulate chemical processes that influence our health and wellbeing. "Vibrational medicine," also called energy medicine, strives to use the energy generated by and around a person's body to optimize their health.

Affirmations and the Law of Attraction

Affirmations are simply positive statements made in the present tense that impact our conscious and subconscious minds. By saying them regularly, we can increase our vibrational frequency. The Law of Attraction states that "like attracts like." Therefore, when you begin vibrating in a higher, more positive frequency, you will start attracting higher-vibrational people and opportunities into your life.

Positive affirmations are a "self-talk approach" for creating a positive, motivating outlook on life while becoming your authentic self. We are more easily able to connect with our authentic selves when our vibrations are high. Unfortunately, unhealthy, unsupportive inner dialogue can remain our default mode when we are not vibrating highly.

But what is a vibration? How do you know if you are vibrating highly or not? Well, everything has a vibrational frequency. Quantum physics can illustrate this, but all that's really required is remembering the basics.

Remember atoms and molecules? They come together to create matter in the form of a solid, liquid, or gas. Atoms, the smallest indivisible units of matter, are made of energy and are constantly vibrating. Since atoms are made of vibrating energy, and all matter is made of atoms, all matter is made of energy, and all matter is vibrating. You don't have to see vibrations to know they're there. Have you ever walked into a room and felt its vibe? If you have, you've intuitively sensed whether the people in the room were getting along, were uncomfortable, excited, sad, or happy. When you walk into a room, and it feels a certain way, you've picked up on its vibration. And when you meet a person and immediately feel connected, it's because you are most likely vibrating similarly!

Our vibrations are continually changing, shifting with our moods, health, and according to the energy *that surrounds us.*

We can *choose* whether we would like to vibrate higher or lower than our current state of being. When you vibrate at a lower frequency, it feels heavy, and when you're vibrating at a higher frequency, you feel lighter, at ease, happy, and at peace. Vibrating at a higher frequency feels *good*! Focusing on that which brings us joy and happiness raises our vibrational frequency, and when we get ourselves into a higher vibration, we let go of that which no longer serves us.

When you begin releasing everything that weighs you down to maintain a higher frequency or vibration, you will experience more positive emotions. Feeling good will be your default state of being.

To help you better understand how your feelings vibrate, Abraham-Hicks has created the "emotional guidance scale" below. The feelings listed are ranked from highest to lowest vibrating. They give an idea of how you might be vibrating at any given time:

- Joy/apprehension/empowerment/freedom/love
- Passion
- Enthusiasm/eagerness/happiness
- Positive expectations/belief
- Optimism
- Hopefulness
- Contentment
- Boredom
- Pessimism
- Frustration/irritation/impatience
- Overwhelm
- Disappointment
- Doubt
- Worry
- Blame
- Discouragement
- Anger
- Revenge
- Hatred/rage
- Jealousy
- Insecurity/guilt/unworthiness
- Fear/grief/depression/despair/powerlessness

Affirmations raise your vibration when you're stuck in a low vibrational pattern like fear, worry, anxiety, doubt, and powerlessness. Affirmations are a powerful tool for manifesting change *and* lifting your attitude *at the same time*. Speaking positive affirmations is one of the quickest ways to raise your vibration!

As you continue to use affirmations, your vibration will increase, and you'll notice that you feel happier and more peaceful. You'll begin to attain your goals, fulfill your desires, and attract the people and experiences you want.

Let's Get High

When we hold highly vibrating thoughts, feelings and behaviors, we naturally start to vibrate accordingly. When we vibrate at a higher frequency, we feel a sense of peace and connectedness to everything. We worry less because we're confident, *knowing* everything in life is as it should be, and getting better in every way.

By speaking affirmations every day, you'll become consciously aware of your thoughts, attitudes, choices, and behaviors. You'll notice where changes are happening and where changes still need to happen. You'll feel more positive energy, and you'll attract more positivity in the form of people and opportunities.

Additional benefits:

- You feel better
- You have a joyful worldview
- You are naturally drawn to people, places, and experiences that bring you positivity and happiness
- You stop attracting people, things, and experiences that get in the way of your growth
- You feel energized
- Other people notice and enjoy being with you

Mindfulness

When implementing any change, you must be aware of the change you want to make throughout the day, every day, for it to be successful. You must *intentionally* commit to making the change every day.

What do you want to change about yourself? Do you have personality traits or characteristics that you don't like, criticize, judge, or loathe? Maybe you have habits or perceived shortcomings that you'd like to give up? Is there an aspect of your life that you want to develop? Your answers to questions like these can give you ideas about the kinds of positive affirmations you can create.

Thoughts Become Things

When we hold low vibrational thoughts and beliefs, we lower our vibration, inevitably hampering our affirmation's likelihood of success. This is because our subconscious minds accept any repeated declaration as truth, even when these affirmations are negative. Be aware of your negative thoughts.

We use affirmations to change the way we think about ourselves. Affirmations remind us of our highest potential, and our vibrational frequency must increase to match that potential. You must raise your vibration to align with your goals when you're manifesting your best life.

We know that affirmations are more likely to work when they vibrate highly. That's because highly vibrating affirmations attract what we've always wanted but believed we couldn't have. If your affirmations don't vibrate highly, rewrite them.

When you've learned how to write and use affirmations correctly, you will start manifesting your goals. As your vibration increases, you'll become aware of your daily thoughts and practices, and you'll begin living in alignment with the life you're trying to create.

As you write and speak your affirmations, focus on gratitude, love (including self-love), optimism, and spiritual guidance. This practice will further increase your vibrational frequency.

After you write an affirmation, take a look at it, say it, and see how it feels. It should vibrate highly. Keep working on it until it does.

To achieve the life you want, you will need to write robust, highly vibrating affirmations, and believe these declarations to already be true. If you don't write your affirmations correctly, saying them can be an absolute waste of time.

Short, Clear, Concrete, Positive and Present Tense

Affirmations that work best are short, clear, concrete, positive, present tense, and highly personal.

Short

Use only a few words in your affirmations to make them easier to remember. To accomplish this, begin with a phrase like:

I am...

I easily...

I joyfully...

I clearly see, hear, do...

I excitedly...

I look forward with joy to...

I look forward to the opportunity that_____provides for_____.

Your affirmations should be authentic, meaning that they feel doable and true for you. Our quantum self (the sub-atomic realm of our consciousness) recognizes the truth within our affirmations.

Looking at the phrases above, notice that they are assertive. If you use words like "I feel," it implies that your affirmation is temporary because *feelings* are temporary. Do you ever *feel* confident when you wear a particular item of clothing? What happens when you take it off? Do you see what I mean? The feeling of confidence may decrease or disappear altogether. When you say "I am," it implies that it's permanent, no matter the time, place, or situation. It says that you OWN IT.

Clear

What is it that you want to achieve? What do you want to change about yourself? Ask yourself questions to find concrete answers to include in your affirmations. For instance:

"How can I _____?" vs. "I can't because _____."

Do you see the difference between these two approaches? Asking questions prompts your mind to start looking for real answers, consciously and unconsciously. Asking questions opens up possibilities. When you tell yourself you can't, it stops your mind from considering solutions. It prevents new ideas from forming. You can see how this would not be a good approach for changing your thoughts, beliefs, and mindset. So think about the goals you want to achieve and ask the questions. Write the first answers that come to mind without censoring or editing. I recommend this approach because the first answers often come from our higher self and are the purest and most confident.

Using your answers, write short affirmational statements that resonate highly with you. Write them as if *the desired outcome has already happened.*

For example: "I have strong intuition, and I trust it."

Concrete

Did you notice that most of the phrases above include an adjective? Do you remember learning about adjectives in school? Adjectives are "picture words" that help to describe something strongly enough to provide a mental visual image. Using only the best adjectives or descriptors means that you will not leave any room for improvement. In other words, your affirmation will state that you're already at the best and highest level of whatever it is you want to achieve. For example, "I joyfully embrace all that life offers me" vs. "I love my life." See what I mean? The first affirmation is much stronger than the second. Another way of saying this is that the first affirmation vibrates higher or has a higher frequency than the second.

It takes practice. You can (and will) rewrite your affirmations many times! You'll rewrite them as many times as you need to make them the best, strongest, and highest vibrational frequencies they can be.

Add some feeling

While your affirmations should avoid the words "I feel," the most powerful affirmations include *outcomes* and your *feelings* about them.

The focus of the affirmation should be the *outcome* you desire, and you should include how you *feel* about that outcome. What is your affirmation focused on? Read it aloud to see where you've put the focus.

Consider these affirmations:

The affirmation "I am not afraid of public speaking" puts the focus on fearfulness. A better way to write it is: "I am relaxed and at ease when speaking in public." This second example puts the focus on the outcome of *feeling at ease*.

The affirmation "I want to eliminate all of my debt" puts the focus on debt.

A better way to write it is: "I enjoy complete financial freedom." It focuses on the outcome of *enjoying financial freedom*.

The affirmation "I support my intellectual growth" focuses on intellectual growth, which is fine, but there is no feeling involved.

Better: "I ecstatically support and love my growing intellect!" puts the focus on the outcome and includes feelings of excitement and love for intellectual growth.

When you say the affirmation, you really need to let yourself feel it. The Law of Attraction states that *feeling* is essential to manifesting anything! Feel it in your heart and feel your vibration increase!

Positive

According to experts, one of the most important things about writing positive affirmations is eliminating all negative words. It makes sense, right? After all, they're called "positive" affirmations. So, any negative words like "not" or "can't" must be avoided. For example, say "I am brave" instead of "I am not afraid." Again, see the difference? "Afraid" is the belief you're trying to eliminate. If you say, "I am not afraid," you're focusing on being afraid! So take out the word "not" and put the focus on the goal. If you say "I am brave," you are focusing on the feeling of bravery.

The change in wording makes a difference to your mind. Make sure you're focusing on *what you want*, not on what you don't want. Your words, and the focus you put on them, will make a difference in the outcome.

"I am not afraid" and "I am brave" are two different thoughts, two different ideas, and two different vibrational frequencies. Try rewording your affirmations and feel the difference for yourself!

Present Tense

We stay in the present tense because our higher self works in the present moment. Start your affirmation by thoughtfully entering into the present tense. Assertively declare that your goal is already the reality.

How Many?

People ask how many affirmations they should use. There's really no correct answer or magic number. The number of affirmations you create depends on how many goals you focus on at one time.

Three for Each

My friend Ellen MaRee is an Intuitive Life Coach who helps people integrate with their authentic selves (Sign up for a free consultation on ellenmaree.com!) She advises writing and saying affirmations in sets of three, increasing the vibration with each one.

For example, if I want to cultivate a worry-free, peaceful life, I might write these three:

1. I am content and enjoy my life. (Good)

2. I cheerily cultivate inner peacefulness and gratitude. (Better)

3. I am ceaselessly connected to the infinite, ancient wisdom of the Universe. I am lovingly provided everything that I need or want. (Best)

The first affirmation is acceptable. It's short, clear, concrete, positive, and present tense, and it will work. It vibrates nicely.

The second one is stronger because of the added adjective "cheerfully," which is a feeling. Affirmations should be feeling statements. Do you feel the difference?

The third affirmation vibrates very highly; it's also short, clear, concrete, positive, and present tense. It has the additional benefit of adjectives that describe the highest level of achievement possible. As you say each of these affirmations in order, can you feel your vibration increasing? This is what you want. Try it with your own affirmations and see if your vibration increases with each one. When it does, you know you've got a set of powerful, highly vibrating affirmational statements.

SAFE AND ACCESSIBLE

When starting a new practice like using affirmations, it's helpful to keep them easily accessible to build the daily habit of using them. Keep them where they're convenient to find. Many people choose to keep them on their phones because they're always within reach. You can even set reminders so you'll remember to say them.

Some people like to write affirmations in a journal or notebook and read them silently. They can even be used as writing prompts; as you think about each affirmation, write about the thoughts and feelings that arise.

Some prefer to write their positive affirmations on index cards or sticky notes and leave them in random places they'll see them at specific times. That wouldn't work for me because I view affirmations as a very personal thing, but this method could work well for some.

I find that affirmations work better for me when I speak them aloud. One of my most profound childhood wounds was the belief that I didn't matter. Not only that I didn't matter, but that nothing I thought, felt, or said mattered, and I often felt invisible, unseen, and unheard. Speaking my affirmations aloud showed me how to use my voice as a form of empowerment and self-validation.

Recap

Listen to your intuition, your inner voice, before you begin writing your affirmations. What is your inner voice telling you? What do you need to work on? Let your internal compass direct the course. Allow the journey to begin because you love yourself.

Your affirmations should be:

- Short
- Clearly stated
- Direct and to the point (concrete)
- Purely positive (no negative words)
- In the present tense
- Focused on what you want to achieve
- The highest level of achievement possible
- Easily accessible

Chapter Four
FOUR FUNDAMENTALS

To be the most potent and effective, Ellen MaRee teaches that these four fundamentals should be part of our daily practice.

Positive affirmations have the most substantial impact when they are used frequently and regularly. This consistency will reinforce the positive thoughts, feelings, and behaviors you're creating. To uncover your authentic self and create the life you want, regularly think positive thoughts to replace the old ways of thinking.

Start by developing a new habit of writing and speaking your affirmations at the same times every day. Say your affirmations first thing in the morning and again before bed. Affirm yourself throughout the day; say them whenever you have an opportunity. The more often you affirm who you are, the faster your mind will begin believing and changing.

When you do this, your daily affirmations practice will become a habit. Each aspect of this routine will begin to flow naturally into the next. As you incorporate this exercise into your day, your vibration will rise. You'll more easily visualize what you want and begin manifesting it.

For the best results, add these four specific fundamentals to your daily affirmations practice.

Intend

When you are intentional, your focus is on the present moment. Before speaking your affirmations, state your intention.

Why do you feel the need to use this affirmation? The answer to this question will tell you more about your intention. Your intention is the *reason* for speaking your affirmation.

Ask yourself:

What do you want to change? What is your role in the current situation? What will your new role be? What are some qualities of your *authentic* self? What is your new, real identity like?

By stating what you intend to accomplish when speaking your affirmations, you declare your commitment to what you want this journey to be about.

"Receiving" what you are asking for should always be one of your intentions.

Tapping

Tapping enthusiasts say that it's possible to increase the strength of affirmations by tapping on your chakras during your daily practice.

Chakras (cakras in Sanskrit) are energy centers in our bodies. They correspond to areas of the nervous system, organs, and other regions that affect emotional and physical wellbeing. There are seven main chakra energy centers in the body.

The idea is that by lightly and systematically tapping along these energy meridians, "stuck" energy and negative emotions will be cleared from the body.

You can learn more about tapping (known as the "Emotional Freedom Technique") at tapping.com. You'll find 13 free videos that teach and demonstrate how to use the tapping technique to free yourself of negative thoughts, feelings, and beliefs.

AFFIRM

Affirmations are a method of reprogramming your mind. Reprogramming is possible because our minds don't differentiate between fantasy and reality. Case in point: have you ever been frightened watching a movie, or maybe you felt moved to tears by a particular scene? Yes? That's because your mind couldn't tell the difference between a make-believe situation and real life.

When you speak your affirmations, you declare and validate who you are when you live as your authentic self.

Speak clearly, assertively, and feel the truth of your statement. If your affirmation doesn't ring true, that indicates that you need to rewrite it. Keep rewriting until it feels true.

Trauma counselor Dr. Christine Gibson advises that when an affirmation doesn't feel factual, no matter how you revise it, add the words "what if" in front of the affirmation and say it as a question. For example, "**What if** I am a loveable person who deserves the care, affection, and respect of others?" Notice how, when you give your mind a question, it starts focusing on finding an answer. Doing this exercise will prompt your intellect to look for answers to the question, and eventually, you may see that the answer is affirmative. Once you're at that point, say the affirmation without the what-if.

Remember, the Law of Attraction states that our vibrational frequency attracts similar frequencies to us. Therefore, every affirmation should resonate highly to begin drawing people, places, and things of a similar vibration.

Ask

When you're done speaking your affirmations, it's time to ask for and visualize what will contribute to becoming your authentic self. These include your authentic self's character traits, morals, and skills.

Make a list of the personality traits, moral convictions, beliefs, skills you desire, and activities that fulfill you. Some examples are: being a great conversationalist, a good decision-maker, having an outgoing personality, being a friend that people want, feeling calm and serene, spending time with loved ones, starting new outdoor activities, enjoying peaceful, loving relationships with your children, and accepting and liking yourself. These are changes you want in your life because they bring joy, and when you experience them, you feel genuine, authentic, and true to yourself.

When it came to asking, I noticed a definite disconnect and some push-back from myself when I asked for what I wanted. I discovered the resistance came from holding onto the "not good enough's," the feelings and beliefs that I wasn't worthy, didn't matter, and I should never ask for anything. I'd always believed that I should simply accept whatever life brought because I didn't have or deserve the power to influence my life.

I looked at this push-back, and I began to question those old beliefs. As I did, I started to comprehend that people are dynamic and changeable. I was able to change my inner dialogue from unhelpful and unsupportive to helpful and positive by using affirmations. I began to reframe my ideas about who I am and why I'm here. I learned that I could co-create my best life by ridding myself of limiting beliefs and asking for and visualizing what I wanted. These mental transformations were a game-changer.

So, visualize yourself doing or having the things you want; relationships, personality traits, morals, beliefs, perspectives, and skills. Ask your higher power for them specifically. Notice how it feels. You have to feel it! What did you observe? If there's push-back, I invite you to look at it closely to discover what it means and work through it.

Gratitude, Gratitude, Gratitude

You've stated your intentions and spoken your affirmations in a clear, assertive voice, allowing yourself to bask in their truth, increasing your vibration. You've asked for and visualized the changes you want to make for yourself. Now it's time to thank your higher power for helping you to connect with your authentic self and creating the life you desire.

Start by observing how it feels to express gratitude for everything you have right now. Create a gratitude list of the things you are grateful for at this moment. Focus on the specific people, relationships, events, opportunities, places, and things in your life. Now include gratitude for your authentic self and the ability to forgive yourself, love yourself, nurture yourself, and heal. Really feel thankful and appreciative for everything that comes to mind. You may notice your vibration intensifying.

When you're feeling and focusing on gratitude, be mindful. Center and ground yourself.

Celebrate your wins, and add them to your gratitude list every day. Your list is a dynamic, ever-changing document. Each day and night, refer to your gratitude list and add other things for which you are appreciative: interactions, people, opportunities, transformation, coworkers, clients, family members, friends, pets, neighbors, helpers. Every time you read through your list, you'll notice it's growing, and you'll be reminded that your affirmations are working.

Adding to and reviewing a gratitude list is an enjoyable, vibration-strengthening way to start each day and finish every evening. I hope you give it a try!

Chapter Five
WHO YOU ARE, REALLY

Your Authentic Self

Your authentic self is who you are, regardless of your profession, influence, race, ethnicity, religion, family, or income. It is what is left when you strip away all of the labels, titles, possessions, and all the "things" that you've connected to yourself as part of your identity.

Suppose you take away each of these things: your job, business or profession, all of your friends, followers on social networks, marital status, family, education, degrees, awards, bank accounts, social and financial situation, vehicles, body, state of health, clothing, jewelry, stocks, bonds, real estate, shoes, hair, branding, EVERYTHING. What is left?

What is left is YOU, your authentic self.

Living as your authentic self means that you don't care what others think of you or about you; you are *you* in all settings and situations. You remain true to yourself in your thoughts, words, and behavior no matter what is occurring around you or with the people in your life.

POSITIVE AFFIRMATIONS VS. CODEPENDENCY

Suppose we don't frequently remind ourselves of who we are and what we want. In that case, we can easily slip back into living our lives on other's terms and lose our true identities. We become other-focused and work to become what someone else wants us to be. This loss of self is at the core of codependency, enabling, and people-pleasing.

Positive affirmations are the opposite of codependency. By speaking positive affirmations, we are reminded that we are powerful, that we matter, that we are worthy and that we already have the answers we seek. When we stand in this truth, *our truth*, we feel this. We *know* this.

Many of the affirmations in this book will help diminish codependent thinking and behaving. You'll notice that many can also be applied to more than one topic and are repeated in subsequent chapters of this book.

I've heard it said that "damnation is the discontinuation of growth and development." We may not know where we're going, but let's not go back to where we've been. Keep growing, keep learning, keep moving forward, keep healing. Learn to trust in the ebb and flow of life and in yourself.

Chapter Six
DEALING WITH TOXIC PEOPLE

We know that those on the narcissistic spectrum or afflicted with narcissistic personality disorder (NPD) have a distorted self-image. These individuals are often described as "challenging" to interact (or have a relationship) with. They are defensive, condescending, and usually believe that they "know everything." They like the appearance of prestige and power and are inclined to criticize and shame. They are manipulative. They protect their sense of self at any cost, including using aggression or physical abuse. Their emotions are often unstable, intense, and out of proportion to the situation at hand, and they display a noticeable lack of empathy or caring about others' feelings or wellbeing.

The Dilemma

There's debate about whether narcissists feel emotional empathy and whether they feel guilt or remorse.

If you see someone crying, and it makes you feel sad, you're experiencing emotional empathy.

Emotional empathy requires:

- Feeling the same emotion as another person (for example, seeing someone embarrass themselves and feeling embarrassed for them.)

- Feeling distressed in response to another person's feelings

- Feeling compassion for another person

An emotionally unstable parent who feels no emotional empathy will verbally and emotionally abuse their children. They impulsively change the children's roles within the family. The children take turns being devalued and idealized by the ill parent. Idealizing includes praising, over-attentiveness, and boasting. Types of devaluing include criticizing, blaming, shaming, lying about, lying to, intentionally frightening, projecting, and gaslighting.

Like satellites, every family member revolves around this explosive, unbalanced person, doing what they can to remain in good standing, to avoid further chaos and abuse.

Most narcissists will never see or question their role in hurtful interactions. They won't know the harm they've done to their children. They will never take responsibility for the relationship damage or emotional wounds they've inflicted. Most don't seek treatment and will never benefit from a professional diagnosis because they believe their problems are caused by others. They are blamers.

This dysfunctional dynamic leaves those orbiting the narcissist burdened with unnecessary guilt and shame and left feeling insecure, distrustful, and fearful.

Building self-confidence, self-esteem, and self-trust and creating a sense of personal power will benefit these individuals greatly in their recovery journeys.

The following affirmations will help you to cope with selfish, mean-spirited, challenging, or toxic individuals.

Affirmations to Counteract Negativity

- I am grateful for all of the love that is in my life.
- I accept that others love the best way they know how.
- I let go of the need for others to validate me.
- I value myself.
- I am human. It's OK to be imperfect.
- I listen when my heart talks to me.
- I acknowledge and protect my personal power.
- Today I take care of myself.
- I listen to my wise higher self.
- I allow others the freedom and dignity to learn from their mistakes.
- My boundaries are a form of self-love.
- I focus on what I can control, and I release the rest.
- This is stressful, so I take extra good care of myself today.
- I am a loveable person who deserves the care, affection, and respect of others.
- I make healthy choices for myself.
- I am getting through this by making healthy choices.
- It's OK for me to be afraid and courageous at the same time.
- I am doing the best that I can, and that's all I ask of myself.
- I ask for help when I am struggling.
- I have easy, mutually accepting relationships.

- I take work breaks to rest or have fun.
- I am stronger than I thought.
- I lean on others for support, and I am lovingly supported.
- I value myself.
- I rely on my higher power for strength and guidance.
- I easily dial-up my confidence anytime I want.
- I acknowledge the things that I like about myself and add to that list regularly.
- I am resilient.
- I am unaffected by other's negativity.
- I see the good things in myself.
- I am intelligent and use my mind to make my life better.
- I have strong intuition, and I trust it even if I don't like what it tells me.
- When I see red flags occurring in people or relationships, I pay attention to them and respond accordingly.
- I ask for clarification when I am confused.
- I attract mentally and emotionally stable people.
- I attract kind and caring people.
- I trust my mind.
- I trust my decisions.
- I trust my senses of sight, hearing, smell, taste, and touch.
- I know which responsibilities are mine and which are not.

- I balance my empathy for others with personal boundaries and self-care.
- I am whole.
- I am in control of my thoughts and actions
- I am in control of my triggers.
- I am a survivor and healed warrior.
- Today I give myself the freedom to make an error and know that it does not affect my worth as a human being.
- My relationships are respectful and peaceful.
- I am excitedly hopeful. Healing is possible.
- I am connected with my authentic self.
- I express myself confidently.
- I hear my intuition and inner wisdom, and I listen.
- I am well and worthy.
- I let go of controlling or manipulating others.
- I know and trust my own mind.
- I stand in my truth, and I am heard.
- Only I can determine my self-worth.
- I easily see a person's authentic self, and I embrace what they're showing me.
- My words are kind and loving.
- I speak highly about _____, and they speak highly of me.
- Now is the time to step into my power.
- I am loved, loving and lovable.
- I can do hard things.
- I am and always have been worthy.

- I am and always have been good enough.
- I focus on what's happening right now.
- I let go of responsibilities that are not mine.
- I am smart and capable.
- When I have a problem, I focus on solutions.
- People like me.
- I am naturally relaxed and confident.
- I am safe and secure.
- I am emotionally and physically strong.
- When I enter a room, I am poised and self-confident.
- I allow peace into my life.
- I use my voice to protect myself.
- I effectively communicate my needs and desires.
- I make a positive difference in the world.
- I accept that others love the best they can and may be limited in their ability to express love.
- I honor and respect myself.
- I face my problems with courage and trust.
- I let go of control and allow life to unfold.
- I ask for what I want.
- I clearly state my expectations.
- I dare to be imperfect.
- My voice empowers me.
- I am centered and focused.
- I am capable and can easily handle anything that comes my way.
- I am unaffected by the desires of others.
- I trust my inner voice.

- I let go of those not headed where I am going as a form of self-respect.
- I am unaffected by other's judgments.
- I repair relationships only with those willing to take their share of responsibility for what went wrong.
- Other's words have no power over me.
- Every decision I make is right for me.
- All is well in my life.
- I no longer live within the limitations of another's insecurity.
- I allow others the dignity of making their own choices.
- I let go of everything that does not promote positivity in my life.
- I am nourished and supported by my higher power.
- I cultivate inner peacefulness and gratitude.
- I am connected to the infinite ancient wisdom of the universe, which guides me.
- I let go and move on quickly and easily.
- I trust my higher power to nourish and support me.
- I easily let go of the need to understand everyone and everything.
- I let go of the need for others to understand me.
- I choose to trust and be open to all possibilities.
- I have confidence in myself.
- I easily allow others their own journey.
- I am grounded and centered.
- I easily cultivate a group of like-minded people.
- I gain confidence with every action I take.

- Only good will come from this situation. I am safe.
- I am safe and secure at all times.
- I have everything I need. I am safe and loved.
- I give my time and energy to those who deserve it.
- I allow the negative comments or behaviors of others to bounce off me.
- I release the negativity of toxic people.
- I am happy and positive no matter who I am around.
- I let go of those who don't support and care about me.
- I know who deserves an explanation, who deserves an answer, and who deserves no response at all.

My Healing Affirmations

- _____
- _____
- _____
- _____
- _____
- _____
- _____
- _____
- _____
- _____
- _____
- _____
- _____
- _____
- _____
- _____
- _____
- _____

Chapter Seven
STAND IN YOUR POWER

All narcissists brag, take advantage of people, and speak negatively about others to make themselves feel superior. *Overt* narcissists do these things in distinct, noticeable ways. They attract attention by over-dressing, dressing provocatively, talking too loudly, wearing attention-getting makeup, hairstyles, accessories, or driving flashy cars. They require admiration, and if they don't get it, they may react with rage, ridicule, mockery, or humiliation. They use charm and flattery to manipulate others into liking them even though they're arrogant and proud. They see others as insignificant or as competitors and feel entitled to special treatment.

COVERT NARCISSISTIC MOTHERS

If you find yourself denying, minimizing, or making excuses for your mother's behavior, that's a red flag. If you feel like a detective looking for reasons to explain things she does or says, it could be that she's a covert narcissist.

Covert narcissists are subtle and can be tricky to identify. They are cautious and reserved in how they get their narcissistic supply, the admiration, attention, or emotional reaction that narcissists need to keep their false faces intact. They take this supply from people in their environment. Covert narcissistic moms get their narcissistic supply mainly from *their children.*

When we have a covert narcissist mom, we'll eventually develop feelings of "walking on eggshells" or tip-toeing around to avoid upsetting or angering her. We instinctively know we're not emotionally safe with her. Anything we say or do that displeases her will be remembered and held against us.

Covert narcissist moms often use "exclusionary behaviors," like withholding affection and attention or temporarily withdrawing love and support.

You might notice discrepancies between her words and actions; they don't align. These are called "mixed messages," a type of communication where one individual sends conflicting information to another, either verbally or nonverbally. Mixed messages contribute to the listener being on high alert, edgy, and confused.

All of these feelings and behaviors contribute to feeling a loss of personal power. Everyone is born with personal power. It comes from within. It's important to feel your power to be emotionally healthy.

Owning your power increases your self-confidence and decision-making ability. Your personal power gives you the confidence to create and maintain healthy relationships. It prompts you to speak up for or protect yourself. Your personal power allows you to create and maintain boundaries. It values self-care. It says you matter and that you are worthy.

Reconnecting with your power is essential if your goal is to remove codependent thoughts and behaviors or heal from former abusive or toxic relationships. Use the following affirmations to start feeling your power.

Affirmations For Standing in Your Power

- My personal power is stronger every day.
- I am my own person. I choose how I think and behave.
- I vibrate love to everyone I know.
- I love myself for who I am.
- I am grateful for all of the love that is in my life.
- I love myself unconditionally.
- I accept that others love the best way they know how.
- I use my voice, and I am heard.
- I let go of the need for others to validate me.
- I value myself.
- I am human. It's OK to be imperfect.
- I listen when my heart talks to me.
- I reaffirm for myself that I am on the right path.
- The past is over. I happily focus on the present moment, feeling empowered.
- I am in charge. Today's thoughts create my future.
- I acknowledge and protect my personal power.
- I am safe and free.
- I listen to my wise higher self.
- I allow others the freedom and dignity to learn from their mistakes.
- I allow without judgment.
- My boundaries are a form of self-love.
- I focus on what I can control, and I release the rest.

- This is stressful, so I take extra good care of myself today.
- I make healthy choices for myself.
- I am kind and gentle with myself.
- I am optimistic.
- It's OK for me to be afraid and courageous at the same time.
- I am doing the best that I can, and that's all I ask of myself.
- I allow others to live their lives, and I release the need to worry or control.
- I take work breaks to rest or have fun.
- I am stronger than I thought.
- I find something for which to be grateful every day.
- I value myself.
- I rely on my higher power for strength and guidance.
- I easily dial-up my confidence anytime I want.
- I acknowledge the things that I like about myself and add to that list regularly.
- I am resilient.
- I am unaffected by other's negativity.
- I see the good things in myself.
- When I feel overwhelmed, I choose healthy ways to cope.
- I am intelligent and use my mind to make my life better.
- I have strong intuition, and I trust it even if I don't like what it tells me.

- When I see red flags occurring in people or relationships, I pay attention to them and respond accordingly.
- I ask for clarification when I am confused.
- My life gets better every day.
- When I slip up, I forgive myself and get back on track immediately.
- I trust my mind.
- I trust my decisions.
- My self-talk is strictly positive.
- I trust my senses of sight, hearing, smell, taste, and touch.
- I know which responsibilities are mine and which are not.
- I balance my empathy for others with personal boundaries and self-care.
- I am whole.
- I am grateful for my ongoing personal development.
- I can, and I will.
- I heal more every day.
- I am in control of my thoughts and actions.
- I am in control of what I think and how I feel.
- I am in control of my triggers.
- I see my relationships improve as I prioritize my self-care.
- I am loving, intelligent, and creative, and I make positive changes in my life.
- I am a survivor and healed warrior.

- Today I give myself the freedom to make an error and know that it does not affect my worth as a human being.
- I deserve good things in life.
- I am connected with my authentic self.
- I express myself confidently.
- I hear my intuition and inner wisdom, and I listen.
- I am well and worthy.
- I let go of controlling or manipulating others.
- I know and trust my own mind.
- I stand in my truth, and I am heard.
- Only I can determine my self-worth.
- I easily see a person's authentic self, and I embrace what they're showing me.
- Now is the time to step into my power.
- I can do hard things.
- I am here, I am alive, I am grateful, I am ready.
- I like myself.
- I am and always have been worthy.
- I am and always have been good enough.
- I take pleasure in my personal development.
- I focus on what's happening right now.
- I let go of responsibilities that are not mine.
- I am smart and capable.
- When I have a problem, I focus on solutions.
- People like me.
- I am naturally relaxed and confident.
- I am safe and secure.

- I am emotionally and physically strong.
- When I enter a room, I am poised and self-confident.
- My body language demonstrates that I am sure of myself.
- My appearance demonstrates that I value myself.
- I feel good about spending money on products and services to care for my body and demonstrate that I value myself.
- I take time for myself to rest, relax, unplug or do something that I enjoy.
- I allow peace into my life.
- I use my voice to protect myself.
- I attract joy into my life.
- I effectively communicate my needs and desires.
- I make a positive difference in the world.
- I love who I am, and I love my potential.
- I release my wounds to my higher power.
- I accept that others love the best they can and may be limited in their ability to express love.
- I honor and respect myself.
- I face my problems with courage and trust.
- I allow myself to be childlike.
- I let go of control and allow life to unfold.
- I ask for what I want.
- I clearly state my expectations.
- I dare to be imperfect.
- My voice empowers me.
- Today I create the life I want.

- I am centered and focused.
- I am capable and can easily handle anything that comes my way.
- I am unaffected by the desires of others.
- I embrace my inner child.
- I trust my inner voice.
- I let go of those not headed where I am going as a form of self-respect.
- I am unaffected by other's judgments.
- I repair relationships only with those willing to take their share of responsibility for what went wrong.
- Other's words have no power over me.
- Every decision I make is right for me.
- All is well in my life.
- I no longer live within the limitations of another's insecurity.
- My body achieves what my mind believes.
- I allow others the dignity of making their own choices.
- I let go of everything that does not promote positivity in my life.
- I want for nothing; I have everything I need.
- I allow what I need to come to me.
- I let go and move on quickly and easily.
- I trust my higher power to nourish and support me.
- I easily let go of the need to understand everyone and everything.
- I choose to trust and be open to all possibilities.
- I have confidence in myself.

- I am ready for everything that life offers me.
- I easily allow others their own journey.
- I am grounded and centered.
- I easily cultivate a group of like-minded people.
- I acknowledge my pain, and I release it willingly and easily.
- I acknowledge my anger and release it willingly and easily.
- I gain confidence with every action I take.
- I embrace change. I am the author of my story.
- I am safe and secure at all times.
- I feel safe wherever I am.
- I give my time and energy to those who deserve it.
- I allow the negative comments or behaviors of others to bounce off me.
- I release the negativity of toxic people.
- I am happy and positive no matter who I am around.

My Healing Affirmations

- _____
- _____
- _____
- _____
- _____
- _____
- _____
- _____
- _____
- _____
- _____
- _____
- _____
- _____
- _____
- _____
- _____
- _____
- _____

Chapter Eight
HEALING THE FIGHT OR FLIGHT RESPONSE

REMEMBERING THE PAST

If you've read "Lemon Moms: A Guide to Understand and Survive Maternal Narcissism," you know that whenever we experience trauma, a hormone called adrenaline is released from our adrenal glands, just above our kidneys. Adrenaline causes a brain structure called the *amygdala* to create a memory of the traumatic event.

No memories, including traumatic ones, are stored as complete, linear "stories." Memories are stored as bits and pieces of sensory input, visual images, smells, sounds, tastes, or physical contact: they are stored the way our five senses experienced the trauma as it happened. The amygdala moves this information into long-term memory and *connects emotions to the memory*. This process gives our memories of traumatic events *a particular degree of emotional intensity.*

Emotional Regulation

It's no surprise that the amygdala plays a role in developing Complex PTSD, or C-PTSD. Suppose the amygdala is continually on high alert from real or perceived threats. In that case, our emotions won't become self-regulated like they're supposed to. Instead of controlling our emotions when we feel them, our emotions will control us.

When your emotions aren't self-regulated from growing up in a dysfunctional home, you'll respond to old, buried memories with an automatic, knee-jerk behavior called "triggering." When you're triggered, your brain has misinterpreted sensory input from your eyes, ears, nose, mouth, or skin as being dangerous or threatening when it's not. If you continue to live in high-alert, "fight-or-flight" survival mode, you'll likely begin coping in ways that aren't good for you. You may start lying, using drugs, overeating, stealing, or impulse shopping. You'll do whatever it takes to help cope with the unmanageable stress. If this describes you, remember, triggers are unhealed wounds. It's time to discover your triggers and do the work to heal them.

The following affirmations will help diminish the intensity of fight or flight mode when you remember traumatic events.

Affirmations For Calming Fight or Flight

- I have confidence in myself.
- I release past hurts into the universe.
- I am grateful for all of the love that is in my life.
- I accept that others love the best way they know how.
- I let go of the need for others to validate me.
- I listen when my heart talks to me.
- The past is over. I happily focus on the present moment, feeling empowered.
- I acknowledge and protect my personal power.
- I am safe and free.
- I hear, affirm, comfort, and validate my inner child.
- Today I take care of myself.
- I listen to my wise higher self.
- I focus on what I can control, and I release the rest.
- This is stressful, so I take extra good care of myself today.
- I am a loveable person who deserves the care, affection, and respect of others.
- I stay in the present and focus on one day at a time.
- My body and mind need rest to recharge, so I let myself rest without judgment.
- I am kind and gentle with myself.
- I am getting through this by making healthy choices.
- I do everything I can to be physically and emotionally healthy.

- I am optimistic.
- It's OK for me to be afraid and courageous at the same time.
- I am doing the best that I can, and that's all I ask of myself.
- I ask for help when I am struggling.
- I allow others to live their lives and release the need to worry or control.
- I take work breaks to rest or have fun.
- I am stronger than I thought.
- I lean on others for support, and I am lovingly supported.
- I find something for which to be grateful every day.
- I value myself.
- I rely on my higher power for strength and guidance.
- I am resilient.
- When I feel overwhelmed, I choose healthy ways to cope.
- I am intelligent and use my mind to make my life better.
- I have strong intuition, and I trust it even if I don't like what it tells me.
- When I see red flags occurring in people or relationships, I pay attention to them and respond accordingly.
- I ask for clarification when I am confused.
- My life gets better every day.
- When I slip up, I forgive myself and get back on track immediately.

- I trust my mind.
- I trust my decisions.
- My self-talk is strictly positive.
- I trust my senses of sight, hearing, smell, taste, and touch.
- I am whole.
- I am grateful for my ongoing personal development.
- I can, and I will.
- I heal more every day.
- I am in control of what I think and how I feel.
- I am in control of my triggers.
- I am a survivor and healed warrior.
- Today I give myself the freedom to make an error and know that it does not affect my worth as a human being.
- My relationships are respectful and peaceful.
- I release old habits and practice new ones.
- I am connected with my authentic self.
- I express myself confidently.
- I hear my intuition and inner wisdom, and I listen.
- I am well and worthy.
- I let go of controlling or manipulating others.
- I know and trust my own mind.
- My boundaries are a form of self-love.
- Only I can determine my self-worth.
- I easily see a person's authentic self, and I embrace what they're showing me.
- My words are kind and loving.

- I speak highly about _____, and they speak highly of me.
- Now is the time to step into my power.
- I am loved, loving and lovable.
- I can do hard things.
- I like myself.
- I am and always have been worthy.
- I am and always have been good enough.
- I focus on what's happening right now.
- I let go of responsibilities that are not mine.
- I am smart and capable.
- When I have a problem, I focus on solutions.
- People like me.
- I am naturally relaxed and confident.
- I am safe and secure.
- I am emotionally and physically strong.
- My body language demonstrates that I am sure of myself.
- I take time for myself to rest, relax, unplug or do something that I enjoy.
- I allow peace into my life.
- I attract joy into my life.
- I effectively communicate my needs and desires.
- I make a positive difference in the world.
- I love who I am, and I love my potential.
- I release my wounds to my higher power.
- I accept that others love the best they can and may be limited in their ability to express love.

- I honor and respect myself.
- I face my problems with courage and trust.
- I allow myself to be childlike.
- I let go of control and allow life to unfold.
- I clearly state my expectations.
- I dare to be imperfect.
- My voice empowers me.
- Today I create the life I want.
- I am centered and focused.
- I am capable and can easily handle anything that comes my way.
- I am unaffected by the desires of others.
- I embrace my inner child.
- I trust my inner voice.
- I let go of those not headed where I am going as a form of self-respect.
- I am unaffected by other's judgments.
- I repair relationships only with those willing to take their share of responsibility for what went wrong.
- Other's words have no power over me.
- All is well in my life.
- I no longer live within the limitations of another's insecurity.
- I let go of everything that does not promote positivity in my life.
- I am nourished and supported by my higher power.
- I am content with and enjoy my life.
- I cultivate inner peacefulness and gratitude.

- I surrender to the plans my higher power has in store for me.
- I allow what I need to come to me.
- I let go and move on quickly and easily.
- I trust my higher power to nourish and support me.
- I easily let go of the need to understand everyone and everything.
- I let go of the need for others to understand me.
- I choose to trust and be open to all possibilities.
- I have confidence in myself.
- I am ready for everything that life offers me.
- I easily allow others their own journey.

My Healing Affirmations

- _____
- _____
- _____
- _____
- _____
- _____
- _____
- _____
- _____
- _____
- _____
- _____
- _____
- _____
- _____
- _____
- _____
- _____

Chapter Nine
FEELING VALIDATED

NOT GOOD ENOUGH CODEPENDENTS

If our mothers parented by blaming, shaming, humiliating, intimidating, manipulating, mocking, and lying, we felt confused, rejected, and not "good enough" during much of our childhoods.

Growing up like this means that we repeatedly got the message that everybody else's needs, especially our mother's, were most important. We became watchers and fixers, focusing on her, and in the three-ring circus that was our home, we jumped through whatever hoops she offered.

As adults, we remain action-takers and "fixers," attempting to control outcomes and solve other people's problems. We take responsibilities that aren't ours, and we may get a lot of satisfaction from acquiring such projects. We are "helpers," putting our needs and desires last if we acknowledge them at all. We feel unloved and resentful, and we don't know why.

INVISIBLE AND SILENT

Growing up in an oppressive environment meant that we weren't allowed to freely express ourselves or ask questions because our mothers weren't interested, or it didn't feel safe. We learned that "being quiet" and suppressing our feelings was a safer way to live. As adults, it is difficult for us to talk about anything personal, have challenging discussions, or let ourselves be vulnerable, and we avoid conflict at all costs.

We became adults who willingly, though unintentionally, serve as the dumping ground for other's emotional garbage. Though we don't like it, we might unconsciously believe we don't deserve anything better than the kind of treatment we endured as kids.

Remaining silent, suppressing feelings, avoiding vulnerability, and believing we don't deserve respect, kindness or love are more aspects of codependency, the disappearing self.

ON BEING SEEN AND HEARD

Validation is the act of recognizing or affirming someone's feelings or thoughts *as sound or worthwhile*. The act of validating is an essential aspect of parenting because it opens the door for safe communication. Feeling heard and understood allows people to *trust*, which is a cornerstone of every relationship, especially between mothers and their children.

Validation is a nonjudgmental and supportive action that requires *emotional empathy*. Ah, yes. The thing that narcissists lack.

If our mothers don't "see" us as individuals with thoughts, feelings, and goals of our own, we may think, feel, and believe that we don't matter.

A validating mother hears what her child is saying and understands that the child has independent emotions and thoughts that may not align with her own. She considers them to be legitimate, even if she disagrees.

Suppose we establish the mindset that we don't matter or that it's OK to be mistreated, unloved, or ignored. In that case, we never learn how to *validate ourselves*. As adults, we don't know how to acknowledge our positive characteristics or personal and professional accomplishments. If we haven't experienced what it's like to be treated as a unique being who matters, we won't believe that *we matter*. We won't learn how to identify emotions, and we risk developing unhealthy coping mechanisms. We've seen that when our emotional, psychological, or physical needs continue to go unmet, we often find harmful or maladaptive ways to get by.

Your worth is not about "doing" or "owning." Your worth comes from the fact that you exist.

Talking With Your Mother

If you feel apprehensive or awkward at the thought of having a serious talk with your mother, it's a signal that you feel unsafe to some degree. Remember, your intuition is there to protect you. It's important to acknowledge what your intuition suggests without judging or assigning any kind of value, such as "bad" or "wrong." Instead, validate yourself by accepting your feelings about talking with your mother. Accept that you have reason to feel the way you do. Recognize that what you sense is valid and honor that.

The Fantasy

As you know by now, if your mother is a narcissist, then it's improbable that you'll be able to have that heart-to-heart conversation with her that you've always longed for. You know the one: where you have a cup of tea or coffee together and just visit peacefully, enjoying each other's company. In your fantasy, you feel lighthearted, and being with her feels easy. You laugh, and you feel safe and comfortable. In your imaginary visit, your mother doesn't judge you, criticize, or make barbed comments. You don't need to justify and defend your every thought, feeling, or choice. In your fantasy, your mother accepts and supports you. She hears you, sees you, and you feel as though you matter a great deal. You feel secure in knowing she's got your back.

Those of us with narcissistic mothers have those kinds of fantasies. In recovery, we learn to accept that she's simply not capable of this kind of emotional connection, and we begin to let that idea go. In healing, we realize that there are always others who want an emotional connection with us, and we nurture *those* relationships.

The following affirmations will help you begin affirming yourself, validating that you matter and are worthy of love, life, and happiness.

Affirmations for Self-Validation

- I am grateful for all of the love that is in my life.
- I love myself unconditionally.
- I use my voice, and I am heard.
- I let go of the need for others to validate me.
- I value myself.
- I am human. It's OK to be imperfect.
- I listen when my heart talks to me.
- I reaffirm for myself that I am on the right path.
- I am in charge. Today's thoughts create my future.
- I acknowledge and protect my personal power.
- I hear, affirm, comfort, and validate my inner child.
- I easily attract _____.
- I listen to my wise higher self.
- I allow without judgment.
- I focus on what I can control, and I release the rest.
- This is stressful, so I take extra good care of myself today.
- I am a loveable person who deserves the care, affection, and respect of others.
- I stay in the present and focus on one day at a time.
- I am kind and gentle with myself.
- I am getting through this by making healthy choices.
- It's OK for me to be afraid and courageous at the same time.
- I am doing the best that I can, and that's all I ask of myself.

- I ask for help when I am struggling.
- I have easy, mutually accepting relationships.
- I am stronger than I thought.
- I find something for which to be grateful every day.
- I rely on my higher power for strength and guidance.
- I easily dial-up my confidence anytime I want.
- I acknowledge the things that I like about myself and add to that list regularly.
- I am resilient.
- When I feel overwhelmed, I choose healthy ways to cope.
- I am kind and empathetic.
- I am intelligent and use my mind to make my life better.
- I am a caring person, and people care about me.
- I am compassionate and show my compassion in a variety of ways.
- I have strong intuition, and I trust it even if I don't like what it tells me.
- When I see red flags occurring in people or relationships, I pay attention to them and respond accordingly.
- I ask for clarification when I am confused.
- I attract mentally and emotionally stable people.
- I attract kind and caring people.
- My life gets better every day.
- When I slip up, I forgive myself and get back on track immediately.
- I trust my mind.

- I trust my decisions.
- My self-talk is strictly positive.
- I trust my senses of sight, hearing, smell, taste, and touch.
- I know which responsibilities are mine and which are not.
- I balance my empathy for others with personal boundaries and self-care.
- I am whole.
- I am grateful for my ongoing personal development.
- I can, and I will.
- I heal more every day.
- I am in control of my thoughts and actions.
- I am loving, intelligent, and creative, and I make positive changes in my life.
- I am a survivor and healed warrior.
- My personal power is stronger every day.
- I am my own person. I choose how I think and behave.
- I vibrate love to everyone I know.
- I love myself for who I am.
- I accept that others love the best way they know how.
- The past is over. I happily focus on the present moment, feeling empowered.
- I am safe and free.
- Today I take care of myself.
- I am compassionate and empathetic.
- I allow others the freedom and dignity to learn from their mistakes.

- My boundaries are a form of self-love.
- I make healthy choices for myself.
- My body and mind need rest to recharge, so I let myself rest without judgment.
- I do everything I can to be physically and emotionally healthy.
- I am optimistic.
- I allow others to live their lives and release the need to worry or control.
- I take work breaks to rest or have fun.
- I lean on others for support, and I am lovingly supported.
- I value myself.
- I am unaffected by other's negativity.
- I see the good things in myself.
- Today I give myself the freedom to make an error and know that it does not affect my worth as a human being.
- I deserve good things in life.
- My relationships are respectful and peaceful.
- I am connected with my authentic self.
- I express myself confidently.
- I hear my intuition and inner wisdom, and I listen.
- I am well and worthy.
- Today I honor and cherish my inner child, who was blameless then and now.
- I let go of controlling or manipulating others.
- I know and trust my own mind.
- I stand in my truth, and I am heard.

- Only I can determine my self-worth.
- Now is the time to step into my power.
- I am loved, loving and lovable.
- I can do hard things.
- I am here, I am alive, I am grateful, I am ready.
- I like myself.
- I am and always have been worthy.
- I am and always have been good enough.
- I take pleasure in my personal development.
- I focus on what's happening right now.
- I let go of responsibilities that are not mine.
- I am smart and capable.
- When I have a problem, I focus on solutions.
- People like me.
- I am naturally relaxed and confident
- I am safe and secure.
- I am emotionally and physically strong.
- When I enter a room, I am poised and self-confident.
- My body language demonstrates that I am sure of myself.
- My appearance demonstrates that I value myself.
- I feel good about spending money on products and services to care for my body and demonstrate that I value myself.
- I take time for myself to rest, relax, unplug or do something that I enjoy.
- I allow peace into my life.
- I use my voice to protect myself.

- I attract joy into my life.
- I effectively communicate my needs and desires.
- I make a positive difference in the world.
- I love who I am, and I love my potential.
- I accept that others love the best they can and may be limited in their ability to express love.
- I honor and respect myself.
- I face my problems with courage and trust.
- I allow myself to be childlike.
- I let go of control and allow life to unfold.
- I ask for what I want.
- I clearly state my expectations.
- I dare to be imperfect.
- My voice empowers me.
- Today I create the life I want.
- I am centered and focused.
- I am capable and can easily handle anything that comes my way.
- I am unaffected by the desires of others.
- I embrace my inner child.
- I trust my inner voice.
- I let go of those not headed where I am going as a form of self-respect.
- I am unaffected by other's judgments.
- I repair relationships only with those willing to take their share of responsibility for what went wrong.
- Other's words have no power over me.
- Every decision I make is right for me.

- All is well in my life.
- I no longer live within the limitations of another's insecurity.
- My body achieves what my mind believes.
- I allow others the dignity of making their own choices.
- I let go of everything that does not promote positivity in my life.
- I am nourished and supported by my higher power.
- I am content with and enjoy my life.
- I cultivate inner peacefulness and gratitude.
- I am connected to the infinite ancient wisdom of the universe, which guides me.
- I want for nothing; I have everything I need.
- I surrender to the plans my higher power has in store for me.
- I allow what I need to come to me.
- I let go and move on quickly and easily.
- I trust my higher power to nourish and support me.
- I easily let go of the need to understand everyone and everything.
- I let go of the need for others to understand me.
- I choose to trust and be open to all possibilities.
- I have confidence in myself.
- I am ready for everything that life offers me.
- I easily allow others their own journey.
- I am grounded and centered.
- I easily cultivate a group of like-minded people.

- I acknowledge my pain, and I release it willingly and easily.
- I acknowledge my anger and release it willingly and easily.
- I gain confidence with every action I take.
- I embrace change. I am the author of my story.
- Everything is working for my highest good.
- I belong. I know that I am safe.
- I have everything I need.
- I release the negativity of toxic people.
- I am happy and positive no matter who I am around.
- I let go of those who don't support and care about me.
- I accept and value myself exactly as I am.

My Healing Affirmations

- _____
- _____
- _____
- _____
- _____
- _____
- _____
- _____
- _____
- _____
- _____
- _____
- _____
- _____
- _____
- _____
- _____

Chapter Ten
WORKING THROUGH NARCISSISM AWARENESS

A Special Kind of Grief

If you've been affected by your mother's diagnosed or suspected narcissism, you can do recovery work to move forward to a healthier mindset and life. You can learn to set healthy boundaries, feel safe, and lose the need to control people and outcomes. You can begin prioritizing yourself without feeling guilty. Positive, healing affirmations will help.

When I first entered into Narcissism Awareness Grief, I slowly became aware of how my mother's illness affected me. I felt a combination of shock, denial, and disbelief. I felt a sense of overwhelming sadness that kept me focused on my childhood and my resentment.

To begin the healing process, I needed to progress through each stage of my grief and finally move into acceptance. It took time. To recover, you must be willing to give yourself unlimited, unpressured time, allowing each step to unfold at its own pace.

As I grasped the *impact* my mother's cruelty had on me, I felt a gamut of emotions—including rage.

When we discover that the traumatic lifestyle we've endured as children has an actual name, it can be a massive relief. There's an initial rush of validation, and we suddenly realize that we're not alone, that we're not crazy, and that we haven't imagined it. Narcissistic trauma and abuse are real things, and we can recover from them.

Your mother's perspective of you is *her* problem; it has nothing to do with you. It has to do with her faulty thinking and perception and not any shortcomings within yourself. As you begin processing these facts, you may start feeling a colossal torrent of conflicting emotions, and you may be confused. As you further acknowledge this new way of perceiving and understanding your mother, you may begin to realize that your mother's worldview is dysfunctional. There is nothing—and there never was—anything inherently wrong with you, as you may have been led to believe.

Awakening

Narcissism Awareness Grief (NAG) begins when you become aware of your mother's illness and realize how it impacted you.

Much like the famous Kubler-Ross "five stages of grief" model, there are several stages of Narcissism Awareness Grief. They're not linear; they're not experienced in any particular order. We can go back and forth between the stages throughout the process of grieving. But every step must be experienced before we can get to the final stage, which is "acceptance." It's also possible to become stuck in any phase for any length of time and never enter into acceptance.

The Stages:

1. Denial
2. Anger
3. Bargaining
4. Depression
5. Rewriting
6. Acceptance

As we feel and do the work necessary to progress through the stages, the last piece, acceptance, comes pretty organically.

When we get to acceptance, we're finally able to accept our mother's narcissism as the permanent disability it is. We see her narcissism as a revelation of sorts. There's an exciting feeling of *freedom* when we understand that we don't have any responsibility or the ability to change her. We're finally able to reframe our childhoods as resulting from *her illness*, not shortcomings within us. And we finally begin to let go of the effects of our dysfunctional childhoods.

We welcome the understanding that narcissists don't change, which makes them very predictable. Now, we can anticipate our mother's behavior, making interacting with her feel safer or more tolerable. As our expectations change, we may experience a sense of peace we never thought possible. We can determine what kind and how much exposure we will subject ourselves to, and we can plan accordingly. Some of us may decide to have no contact at all, and some may choose to have limited contact with strict enforceable boundaries

You may be feeling denial, fear, confusion, shame, rejection, loneliness, abandonment, or any number and combination of emotions as you progress through NAG. These feelings are all an expected part of acknowledging what's happened. The grieving process begins with feeling the feelings.

For more in-depth information about Narcissism Awareness Grief, read "Lemon Moms: A Guide to Understand and Survive Maternal Narcissism."

Affirmations for Working Through Narcissism Awareness Grief

- I always mattered, but my mother couldn't see it or acknowledge it.
- I accept that pain is a part of my growth and personal development.
- I love myself unconditionally.
- I accept that others love the best way they know how.
- The past is over. I happily focus on the present moment, feeling empowered.
- I am in charge. Today's thoughts create my future.
- I acknowledge and protect my personal power.
- I am safe and free.
- I hear, affirm, comfort, and validate my inner child.
- Today I take care of myself.
- I listen to my wise higher self.
- I focus on what I can control, and I release the rest.
- This is stressful, so I take extra good care of myself today.
- I stay in the present and focus on one day at a time.
- My body and mind need rest to recharge, so I let myself rest without judgment.
- I am kind and gentle with myself.
- I am getting through this by making healthy choices.
- I do everything I can to be physically and emotionally healthy.
- I am optimistic.

- It's OK for me to be afraid and courageous at the same time.
- I am doing the best that I can, and that's all I ask of myself.
- I ask for help when I am struggling.
- I take work breaks to rest or have fun.
- I lean on others for support, and I am lovingly supported.
- I find something for which to be grateful every day.
- I rely on my higher power for strength and guidance.
- I am resilient.
- I am unaffected by other's negativity.
- When I feel overwhelmed, I choose healthy ways to cope.
- I ask for clarification when I am confused.
- I attract kind and caring people.
- My life gets better every day.
- I trust my mind.
- My self-talk is strictly positive.
- I trust my senses of sight, hearing, smell, taste, and touch.
- I know which responsibilities are mine and which are not.
- I balance my empathy for others with personal boundaries and self-care.
- I heal more every day.
- I am a survivor and healed warrior.

- Today I give myself the freedom to make an error and know that it does not affect my worth as a human being.
- I release old habits and practice new ones.
- I am excitedly hopeful. Healing is possible.
- I am connected with my authentic self.
- I express myself confidently.
- I hear my intuition and inner wisdom, and I listen.
- I am well and worthy.
- Today I honor and cherish my inner child, who was blameless then and now.
- Now is the time to step into my power.
- I am loved, loving and lovable.
- I can do hard things.
- I focus on what's happening right now.
- When I have a problem, I focus on solutions.
- I am naturally relaxed and confident.
- I am safe and secure.
- I am emotionally and physically strong.
- I take time for myself to rest, relax, unplug or do something that I enjoy.
- I allow peace into my life.
- I effectively communicate my needs and desires.
- I release my wounds to my higher power.
- I accept that others love the best they can and may be limited in their ability to express love.
- My voice empowers me.
- Today I create the life I want.

- I am centered and focused.
- I am unaffected by the desires of others.
- I embrace my inner child.
- I trust my inner voice.
- I let go of those not headed where I am going as a form of self-respect.
- I am unaffected by other's judgments.
- I repair relationships only with those willing to take their share of responsibility for what went wrong.
- Other's words have no power over me.
- I no longer live within the limitations of another's insecurity.
- My body achieves what my mind believes.
- I let go of everything that does not promote positivity in my life.
- I allow what I need to come to me.
- I let go and move on quickly and easily.
- I trust my higher power to nourish and support me.
- I easily let go of the need to understand everyone and everything.
- I choose to trust and be open to all possibilities.
- I am ready for everything that life offers me.
- I easily allow others their own journey.
- I am grounded and centered.
- I easily cultivate a group of like-minded people.
- I acknowledge my pain, and I release it willingly and easily.
- I acknowledge my anger and release it willingly and easily.

- I embrace change. I am the author of my story.
- I am safe and secure at all times.
- Everything is working for my highest good.
- I have everything I need. I am safe and loved.
- I give my time and energy to those who deserve it.
- I allow the negative comments or behaviors of others to bounce off me.
- I am happy and positive no matter who I am around.
- I let go of those who don't support and care about me.

My Healing Affirmations

- _____
- _____
- _____
- _____
- _____
- _____
- _____
- _____
- _____
- _____
- _____
- _____
- _____
- _____
- _____
- _____
- _____
- _____

Chapter Eleven
HEALING BLAME AND REJECTION

For those who haven't experienced maternal narcissism, I think the hardest thing to understand is that narcissistic parents don't see their children as individuals. A narcissistic mother doesn't see her children as independently functioning human beings who have their own thoughts and feelings. She doesn't see their individual personalities or acknowledge their dreams or aspirations.

A narcissistic mother sees her kids as extensions of *herself*. Because of that, she believes that everything her kids do and say reflects on *her*. She makes everything about *her*. The kids are simply satellites who learn at a very young age that they're expected to contribute positively to their mother's self-image. Every decision and every action they take must reflect well on their mother, or there will be ugly consequences.

Projection and Scapegoating

When a narcissistic mother doesn't like aspects of her personality, she unconsciously separates herself from those qualities and then "projects" them onto one of her children. She now sees that child as having those negative traits.

When a narcissistic mom uses projection, there is a risk of neglect, maltreatment, abuse, blame, shame, or even physical violence to the children as a result.

Because narcissistic mothers are so controlling, they need to have reasons that explain undesirable happenings, and they insist on having a person to hold accountable. And because she needs to blame, she'll play the game "whose fault is it? I know it's not mine" (Brenner et al., 2018). This phenomenon is known as scapegoating. The scapegoating practice happens in dysfunctional families, with the role of the scapegoat being either temporary or permanent. The scapegoat is the fall guy. They are the person who gets blamed for offenses and injustices that happen to anyone in the family. Family members, except for the mom, take turns in the scapegoat role. At any given time, the mom determines who the scapegoat is.

Tactics like scapegoating are all attempts to maintain control. When a narcissistic mom feels like she's losing control over her kids, she will often lash out in vengeful ways, subtly or with direct hostility. Narcissistic mothers are highly reactive to any threat or challenge to their power. They have a sense of entitlement, ownership, and possession of their kids.

Scapegoating is a hostile, emotionally damaging practice. It can cause C-PTSD, addiction, depression, resentment, low self-worth, anxiety, panic attacks, unresolved grief, and anger issues, to name a few.

If you were the family scapegoat, the following affirmations will help you to foster feelings of self-acceptance.

Affirmations to Feel Accepted

- I am grateful for all of the love that is in my life.
- I love myself unconditionally.
- I use my voice, and I am heard.
- I let go of the need for others to validate me.
- I value myself.
- I am human. It's OK to be imperfect.
- I listen when my heart talks to me.
- I embrace my new life even when it makes others uncomfortable.
- I am in charge. Today's thoughts create my future.
- I acknowledge and protect my personal power.
- I am safe and free.
- Today I take care of myself.
- I easily attract _____.
- I focus on what I can control, and I release the rest.
- This is stressful, so I take extra good care of myself today.
- I make healthy choices for myself.
- I stay in the present and focus on one day at a time.
- I am kind and gentle with myself.
- I am getting through this by making healthy choices.
- I do everything I can to be physically and emotionally healthy.
- I ask for help when I am struggling.
- I have easy, mutually accepting relationships.

- I allow others to live their lives and release the need to worry or control.
- I am stronger than I thought.
- I lean on others for support, and I am lovingly supported.
- I find something for which to be grateful every day.
- I value myself.
- I easily dial-up my confidence anytime I want.
- I acknowledge the things that I like about myself and add to that list regularly.
- I am unaffected by other's negativity.
- I see the good things in myself.
- When I feel overwhelmed, I choose healthy ways to cope.
- I am kind and empathetic.
- I am intelligent and use my mind to make my life better.
- I am a caring person, and people care about me.
- I am compassionate and show my compassion in a variety of ways.
- I have strong intuition, and I trust it even if I don't like what it tells me.
- When I see red flags occurring in people or relationships, I pay attention to them and respond accordingly.
- I attract mentally and emotionally stable people.
- I attract kind and caring people.
- My life gets better every day.

- When I slip up, I forgive myself and get back on track immediately.
- I trust my mind.
- I trust my decisions.
- My self-talk is strictly positive.
- I trust my senses of sight, hearing, smell, taste, and touch.
- I know which responsibilities are mine and which are not.
- I balance my empathy for others with personal boundaries and self-care.
- I am whole.
- I am grateful for my ongoing personal development.
- I heal more every day.
- I am in control of my thoughts and actions.
- I am in control of what I think and how I feel.
- I am in control of my triggers.
- I see my relationships improve as I prioritize my self-care.
- I am loving, intelligent, and creative, and I make positive changes in my life.
- I am a survivor and healed warrior.
- I deserve good things in life.
- My relationships are respectful and peaceful.
- I release old habits and practice new ones.
- I am connected with my authentic self.
- I express myself confidently.
- I hear my intuition and inner wisdom, and I listen.
- I am well and worthy.

- Today I honor and cherish my inner child, who was blameless then and now.
- I know and trust my own mind.
- My boundaries are a form of self-love.
- Only I can determine my self-worth.
- I easily see a person's authentic self, and I embrace what they're showing me.
- I listen to my wise self.
- I speak highly about _____, and they speak highly of me.
- Now is the time to step into my power.
- I am loved, loving and lovable.
- I can do hard things.
- I am here, I am alive, I am grateful, I am ready.
- I like myself.
- I am and always have been worthy.
- I am and always have been good enough.
- I take pleasure in my personal development.
- I focus on what's happening right now.
- I am smart and capable.
- When I have a problem, I focus on solutions.
- People like me.
- I am naturally relaxed and confident.
- I am safe and secure.
- I am emotionally and physically strong.
- When I enter a room, I am poised and self-confident.
- I take time for myself to rest, relax, unplug or do something that I enjoy.

- I use my voice to protect myself.
- I make a positive difference in the world.
- I love who I am, and I love my potential.
- I release my wounds to my higher power.
- I accept that others love the best they can and may be limited in their ability to express love.
- I honor and respect myself.
- I face my problems with courage and trust.
- I allow myself to be childlike.
- I let go of control and allow life to unfold.
- I ask for what I want.
- I clearly state my expectations.
- I dare to be imperfect.
- My voice empowers me.
- Today I create the life I want.
- I am centered and focused.
- I am capable and can easily handle anything that comes my way.
- I am unaffected by the desires of others.
- I embrace my inner child.
- I trust my inner voice.
- I let go of those not headed where I am going as a form of self-respect.
- I am unaffected by other's judgments.
- I repair relationships only with those willing to take their share of responsibility for what went wrong.
- Other's words have no power over me.
- Every decision I make is right for me.

- All is well in my life.
- I no longer live within the limitations of another's insecurity.
- I allow others the dignity of making their own choices.
- I let go of everything that does not promote positivity in my life.
- I am nourished and supported by my higher power.
- I am content with and enjoy my life.
- I cultivate inner peacefulness and gratitude.
- I am connected to the infinite ancient wisdom of the universe, which guides me.
- I want for nothing; I have everything I need.
- I allow what I need to come to me.
- I let go and move on quickly and easily.
- I easily let go of the need to understand everyone and everything.
- I let go of the need for others to understand me.
- I choose to trust and be open to all possibilities.
- I have confidence in myself.
- I easily allow others their own journey.
- I am grounded and centered.
- I easily cultivate a group of like-minded people.
- I acknowledge my pain, and I release it willingly and easily.
- I acknowledge my anger and release it willingly and easily.
- I gain confidence with every action I take.
- I embrace change. I am the author of my story.

- I am safe and secure at all times.
- Everything is working for my highest good.
- I belong. I know that I am safe.
- I have everything I need. I am safe.
- I give my time and energy to those who deserve it.
- I allow the negative comments or behaviors of others to bounce off me.
- I am happy and positive no matter who I am around.
- I let go of those who don't support and care about me.

My Healing Affirmations

- _____
- _____
- _____
- _____
- _____
- _____
- _____
- _____
- _____
- _____
- _____
- _____
- _____
- _____
- _____
- _____
- _____

Chapter Twelve
HEALING BETRAYAL WOUNDS

Narcissistic Lies

Narcissists lie. A lot.

Narcissistic lying is different than other types of lying. The fundamental difference is motivation. The current theory regarding narcissistic lying is that all narcissistic behaviors, including lying, are unconsciously motivated by shame and driven by previous narcissistic injuries. Lying is central to a narcissist's identity. Still, because all of their experiences are filtered through previous injuries, they'll view the lie as the truth. In his book "The Narcissist You Know," Dr. Joseph Burgo says a narcissist "doesn't see himself as a liar but rather as an embattled defender of the 'truth' as he has come to see it" (Burgo 2016).

A narcissistic mother's lies are a combination of her character traits and life experiences, so there's usually a small "kernel" of truth within each lie. It'll be difficult and confusing to try to find that kernel, but your intuition will tell you it's there. In addition to lying, she'll exaggerate information that makes her look "good," and she'll just as quickly minimize information that has the potential to make her look "bad."

Because narcissists need to believe that they're always correct and never make mistakes, they often have difficulty knowing the difference between lies and the truth. This makes absolute sense if you remember that a narcissist's entire life is a lie because they hide behind a false face. They have grandiose beliefs about their false selves, and they need validation and affirmation to maintain those beliefs.

When narcissists' lies are not believed, there will usually be a narcissistic rage or perhaps a "silent treatment."

Lies destroy trust and respect. They sow seeds of doubt and obliterate our sense of safety. They ruin our faith in the relationship and destroy the liar's credibility. Our own sense of identity may suffer as well.

To recover from deception, first, acknowledge that you trusted an untrustworthy person. There is nothing wrong with you, and you did nothing wrong. You were fooled by someone very good at deception, and you won't let that happen again. You're not a mind reader; you're a trusting person who believed that what you were told was true. Why wouldn't you?

Forgive yourself; grant yourself some grace for trusting an untrustworthy person and believing their lies. You don't have to become a suspicious or distrustful person to avoid future betrayal. Start taking action by learning how to spot deception and begin verifying the things you're told. Use the following affirmations to start healing from betrayal.

Affirmations to Heal Betrayal Wounds

- I am grateful for all of the love that is in my life.
- I use my voice, and I am heard.
- I let go of the need for others to validate me.
- I value myself.
- I listen when my heart talks to me.
- I reaffirm for myself that I am on the right path.
- The past is over. I happily focus on the present moment, feeling empowered.
- I acknowledge and protect my personal power.
- I focus on what I can control, and I release the rest.
- This is stressful, so I take extra good care of myself today.
- I am a loveable person who deserves the care, affection, and respect of others.
- I stay in the present and focus on one day at a time.
- My body and mind need rest to recharge, so I let myself rest without judgment.
- I am getting through this by making healthy choices.
- I do everything I can to be physically and emotionally healthy.
- It's OK for me to be afraid and courageous at the same time.
- I am doing the best that I can, and that's all I ask of myself.
- I ask for help when I am struggling.

- I have easy, mutually accepting relationships.
- I allow others to live their lives and release the need to worry or control.
- I lean on others for support, and I am lovingly supported.
- I value myself.
- I rely on my higher power for strength and guidance.
- I easily dial-up my confidence anytime I want.
- I acknowledge the things that I like about myself and add to that list regularly.
- I am resilient.
- I am unaffected by other's negativity.
- I see the good things in myself.
- When I feel overwhelmed, I choose healthy ways to cope.
- I am intelligent and use my mind to make my life better.
- I am a caring person, and people care about me.
- I have strong intuition, and I trust it even if I don't like what it tells me.
- When I see red flags occurring in people or relationships, I pay attention to them and respond accordingly.
- I ask for clarification when I am confused.
- I attract kind and caring people.
- My life gets better every day.
- I trust my mind.
- I trust my decisions.
- My self-talk is strictly positive.

- I trust my senses of sight, hearing, smell, taste, and touch.
- I know which responsibilities are mine and which are not.
- I balance my empathy for others with personal boundaries and self-care.
- I am whole.
- I am grateful for my ongoing personal development.
- I can, and I will.
- I heal more every day.
- I am in control of my thoughts and actions.
- I am in control of my triggers.
- I am loving, intelligent, and creative, and I make positive changes in my life.
- I am a survivor and healed warrior.
- I deserve good things in life.
- I release old habits and practice new ones.
- I am excitedly hopeful. Healing is possible.
- I am connected with my authentic self.
- I express myself confidently.
- I hear my intuition and inner wisdom, and I listen.
- I am well and worthy.
- Today I honor and cherish my inner child, who was blameless then and now.
- I know and trust my own mind.
- My boundaries are a form of self-love.
- I stand in my truth, and I am heard.
- Only I can determine my self-worth.

- I easily see a person's authentic self, and I embrace what they're showing me.
- I listen to my wise self.
- Now is the time to step into my power.
- I am loved, loving and lovable.
- I can do hard things.
- I am here, I am alive, I am grateful, I am ready.
- I like myself.
- I am and always have been worthy.
- I am and always have been good enough.
- I focus on what's happening right now.
- I let go of responsibilities that are not mine.
- I am smart and capable.
- When I have a problem, I focus on solutions.
- People like me.
- I am naturally relaxed and confident.
- I am safe and secure.
- I take time for myself to rest, relax, unplug or do something that I enjoy.
- I allow peace into my life.
- I use my voice to protect myself.
- I attract joy into my life.
- I effectively communicate my needs and desires.
- I make a positive difference in the world.
- I love who I am, and I love my potential.
- I release my wounds to my higher power.
- I accept that others love the best they can and may be limited in their ability to express love.

- I honor and respect myself.
- I face my problems with courage and trust.
- I allow myself to be childlike.
- I let go of control and allow life to unfold.
- I ask for what I want.
- I clearly state my expectations.
- I dare to be imperfect.
- My voice empowers me.
- Today I create the life I want.
- I am centered and focused.
- I am capable and can easily handle anything that comes my way.
- I am unaffected by the desires of others.
- I trust my inner voice.
- I let go of those not headed where I am going as a form of self-respect.
- I am unaffected by other's judgments.
- I repair relationships only with those willing to take their share of responsibility for what went wrong.
- Other's words have no power over me.
- Every decision I make is right for me.
- All is well in my life.
- I no longer live within the limitations of another's insecurity.
- My body achieves what my mind believes.
- I allow others the dignity of making their own choices.
- I let go of everything that does not promote positivity in my life.

- I am nourished and supported by my higher power.
- I cultivate inner peacefulness and gratitude.
- I am connected to the infinite ancient wisdom of the universe, which guides me.
- I want for nothing; I have everything I need.
- I surrender to the plans my higher power has in store for me.
- I have confidence in myself.
- I am ready for everything that life offers me.
- I easily allow others their own journey.
- I am grounded and centered.
- I easily cultivate a group of like-minded people.
- I acknowledge my pain, and I release it willingly and easily.
- I acknowledge my anger and release it willingly and easily.
- I gain confidence with every action I take.
- I embrace change. I am the author of my story.
- I am safe and secure at all times.
- Everything is working for my highest good.
- I have everything I need. I am safe and loved.
- I give my time and energy to those who deserve it.
- I allow the negative comments or behaviors of others to bounce off me.
- I let go of those who don't support and care about me.

My Healing Affirmations

- _____
- _____
- _____
- _____
- _____
- _____
- _____
- _____
- _____
- _____
- _____
- _____
- _____
- _____
- _____
- _____
- _____
- _____

Chapter Thirteen
HEALING EMOTIONAL ABANDONMENT

Research shows that when we ignore or exclude someone, it activates the same part of their brain as physical pain. Narcissists instinctively know that these manipulative techniques are exceptionally hurtful. Being ignored or excluded are traumatic experiences for those they're imposed upon (Eisenberger et al., 2004).

When a person is actively ignored, it causes such psychological and emotional anguish that it can actually be seen on brain scans (Pune Mirror 2019). For those of us subjected to this form of abuse, the resulting anxiety we felt was triggered by our fear of abandonment. (Saeed, K. 2019).

PUNITIVE SILENCE

Using the "silent treatment" is a way to inflict emotional pain without causing visible evidence. Narcissistic moms love the silent treatment. It's their secret weapon when they want to manipulate and hurt us in a big way.

The silent treatment consists of "hurt and rescue." It may continue for months or even years and is often used to teach a lesson or manipulate behavior (Eisenberger et al., 2004).

As I've noted, a narcissistic mother gets her sense of self through her children. She also needs to protect her self-image and reputation as a loving, caring mother. Her children are a necessary part of her identity, and this is why the silent treatment is so meaningful. It is a fabulous way to keep the children off balance and under her control.

The fear of abandonment is a type of anxiety that can prevent healthy emotional bonds from developing and ruin adult relationships. When we fear abandonment, we may have a series of failed or sabotaged romantic relationships or cling to unhealthy ones. We may fear being alone and require constant reassurance from others to assuage our insecurity. It causes worry, sleep loss, and inability to concentrate. (Imagine trying to learn in school or study for tests while being actively ignored and rejected by a parent!) We go deeper into survival mode with every silent treatment. We may experience panic attacks, appetite loss, binge-eating, racing heartbeat, nightmares, depression, confusion, and obsessive thinking.

The narcissistic mom likes knowing how much she's hurt us with her silent treatment. Our pain demonstrates to her that she is all-powerful and can devastate us if and when she chooses. *It's a great form of narcissistic supply for her.* Our pain is her supply.

Each time we are emotionally abandoned with the silent treatment, we focus more on our mother's behavior and needs. We willingly provide what she needs and do what she wants because we fear we'll be emotionally (or physically) abandoned again. The need to please and appease becomes overblown. This focus on our mother and the need to please her is often the starting point of our codependency.

Every time we go through the silent treatment, we're diminished. Each time we endure active ignoring, we question our self-worth. Our self-esteem and self-image are further eroded, and our fear of abandonment escalates. Despite our accomplishments, acknowledgments, or friendships, we find ourselves desperate for our mother's approval, which, of course, is *always* out of reach.

You can begin overcoming your fear of abandonment by acknowledging your feelings about being alone. Focus on the present, learn new coping skills for anxiety and stress, and use the following affirmations to feel safe.

AFFIRMATIONS TO FEEL SAFE

- I am grateful for all of the love that is in my life.
- I accept that others love the best way they know how. It has nothing to do with me.
- I let go of the need for others to validate me.
- I value myself.
- I am human. It's OK to be imperfect.
- I embrace my new life even when it makes others uncomfortable.
- The past is over. I happily focus on the present moment, feeling empowered.
- I am in charge. Today's thoughts create my future.
- I acknowledge and protect my personal power.
- I am safe and free.
- I hear, affirm, comfort, and validate my inner child.
- Today I take care of myself.
- I easily attract _____.
- I listen to my wise higher self.
- My boundaries are a form of self-love.
- This is stressful, so I take extra good care of myself today.
- I am a loveable person who deserves the care, affection, and respect of others.
- I make healthy choices for myself.
- I stay in the present and focus on one day at a time.
- My body and mind need rest to recharge, so I let myself rest without judgment.

- I am kind and gentle with myself.
- I am getting through this by making healthy choices.
- I do everything I can to be physically and emotionally healthy.
- I am optimistic.
- It's OK for me to be afraid and courageous at the same time.
- I ask for help when I am struggling.
- I have easy, mutually accepting relationships.
- I take work breaks to rest or have fun.
- I lean on others for support, and I am lovingly supported.
- I find something for which to be grateful every day.
- I value myself.
- I rely on my higher power for strength and guidance.
- I easily dial-up my confidence anytime I want.
- I am resilient.
- When I feel overwhelmed, I choose healthy ways to cope.
- I am kind and empathetic.
- I am intelligent and use my mind to make my life better.
- I am a caring person, and people care about me.
- I have strong intuition, and I trust it even if I don't like what it tells me.
- When I see red flags occurring in people or relationships, I pay attention to them and respond accordingly.
- My self-talk is strictly positive.

- I balance my empathy for others with personal boundaries and self-care.
- I am whole.
- I am grateful for my ongoing personal development.
- I can, and I will.
- I heal more every day.
- I am in control of what I think and how I feel.
- I am loving, intelligent, and creative, and I make positive changes in my life.
- I am a survivor and healed warrior.
- My relationships are respectful and peaceful.
- I am connected with my authentic self.
- I express myself confidently.
- I hear my intuition and inner wisdom, and I listen.
- I am well and worthy.
- Today I honor and cherish my inner child, who was blameless then and now.
- I know and trust my own mind.
- I stand in my truth, and I am heard.
- Only I can determine my self-worth.
- I easily see a person's authentic self, and I embrace what they're showing me.
- Now is the time to step into my power.
- I am loved, loving and lovable.
- I can do hard things.
- I am here, I am alive, I am grateful, I am ready.
- I focus on what's happening right now.
- I let go of responsibilities that are not mine.

- People like me.
- I am naturally relaxed and confident.
- I am safe and secure.
- I am emotionally and physically strong.
- I take time for myself to rest, relax, unplug or do something that I enjoy.
- I use my voice to protect myself.
- I attract joy into my life.
- I effectively communicate my needs and desires.
- I love who I am, and I love my potential.
- I accept that others love the best they can and may be limited in their ability to express love.
- I honor and respect myself.
- I face my problems with courage and trust.
- I allow myself to be childlike.
- I let go of control and allow life to unfold.
- I ask for what I want.
- I clearly state my expectations.
- I dare to be imperfect.
- My voice empowers me.
- Today I create the life I want.
- I am centered and focused.
- I am capable and can easily handle anything that comes my way.
- I am unaffected by the desires of others.
- I embrace my inner child.
- I trust my inner voice.

- I let go of those not headed where I am going as a form of self-respect.
- I am unaffected by other's judgments.
- I repair relationships only with those willing to take their share of responsibility for what went wrong.
- Other's words have no power over me.
- Every decision I make is right for me.
- All is well in my life.
- I no longer live within the limitations of another's insecurity.
- I allow others the dignity of making their own choices.
- I let go of everything that does not promote positivity in my life.
- I trust my higher power to nourish and support me.
- I easily let go of the need to understand everyone and everything.
- I let go of the need for others to understand me.
- I choose to trust and be open to all possibilities.
- I easily allow others their own journey.
- I am grounded and centered.
- I gain confidence with every action I take.
- I embrace change. I am the author of my story.
- I am safe and secure at all times.
- Everything is working for my highest good.
- I am safe and protected in every situation.
- My emotions, mind, and spirit are all entirely safe and protected, now and always.
- I belong. I know that I am safe.

- I have everything I need. I am safe. I am loved.
- I give my time and energy to those who deserve it.
- I release the negativity of toxic people.
- I let go of those who don't support and care about me.

My Healing Affirmations

- _____
- _____
- _____
- _____
- _____
- _____
- _____
- _____
- _____
- _____
- _____
- _____
- _____
- _____
- _____
- _____
- _____

Chapter Fourteen
HEALING SHAME

Shaming is a method of control that's interwoven throughout the narcissistic abuse cycle. It is accomplished by using mixed messages, sarcasm, scapegoating, narcissistic rages, gaslighting, silent treatments, and trauma bonding, to name a few. One thing is for sure: you'll find active shaming wherever there is a narcissist.

The shame of enduring mistreatment or abuse from our mothers leaves long-lasting scars.

What Shame Feels Like

Using the word "abuse" to describe our childhood experiences may make us feel uneasy. Describing our childhood as "abusive" may feel like a massive exaggeration or a handy but sad excuse for unresolved personal issues. It may feel like we're saying, "poor me; I'm a helpless victim." It's because the word "abuse" is full of shame.

Shame results from being excluded, belittled, bullied, rejected, or ignored. When I happily played on the floor as a kid and looked over at my mom to share my little-kid-joy and connect with her, she'd scowl at me, and shame moved in.

Our responses to shame-wounds include embarrassment, humiliation, self-disgust, rejection, feeling disliked, unloved, dismissed, or like a failure or "loser."

Shame whispers that everyone is judging you as unforgivingly as you judge yourself. Shame lies. It says that you're unworthy of acceptance or belonging, that you deserve the abusive behavior, the insults, criticisms, rejection, and loneliness. It is shame that says you're not good enough.

Those of us who've experienced traumatic childhood abuses at the hands of our mothers tend to see ourselves in a negative light when comparing ourselves with others.

We may intentionally minimize our painful childhood experiences because we don't want to think of our mothers as "abusers" or ourselves as unwitting targets or victims. Thinking of our mothers as abusers or ourselves as victims can cause us to feel even *more* ashamed than we already do.

Healing shame involves finding healthy ways to meet our needs for connection and acceptance and lovingly nurturing ourselves. Since shame is deeply connected to feeling unworthy, self-affirmation and encouragement are very important. Start using these encouraging, affirming statements to begin healing shame:

Affirmations to Heal Shame

- I am worthy of love, happiness, and fulfillment.
- I have everything I need to be successful.
- I am strong and resilient.
- I am complete and whole.
- I embrace change. I am the author of my story.
- I use my voice, and I am heard.
- I let go of the need for others to validate me.
- I value myself.
- I am human. It's OK to be imperfect.
- I embrace my new life even when it makes others uncomfortable.
- The past is over. I happily focus on the present moment, feeling empowered.
- I am in charge. Today's thoughts create my future.
- I hear, affirm, comfort, and validate my inner child.
- I allow without judgment.
- I focus on what I can control, and I release the rest.
- This is stressful, so I take extra good care of myself today.
- I am a loveable person who deserves the care, affection, and respect of others.
- I make healthy choices for myself.
- I stay in the present and focus on one day at a time.
- I am kind and gentle with myself.
- I am getting through this by making healthy choices.

- I do everything I can to be physically and emotionally healthy.
- I am optimistic.
- It's OK for me to be afraid and courageous at the same time.
- I am doing the best that I can, and that's all I ask of myself.
- I ask for help when I am struggling.
- I have easy, mutually accepting relationships.
- I lean on others for support, and I am lovingly supported.
- I value myself.
- I rely on my higher power for strength and guidance.
- I easily dial-up my confidence anytime I want.
- I acknowledge the things that I like about myself and add to that list regularly.
- I am unaffected by other's negativity.
- I see the good things in myself.
- When I feel overwhelmed, I choose healthy ways to cope.
- I am kind and empathetic.
- I am intelligent and use my mind to make my life better.
- I am a caring person, and people care about me.
- I am compassionate and show my compassion in a variety of ways.
- I ask for clarification when I am confused.
- When I slip up, I forgive myself and get back on track immediately.

- I trust my mind.
- I trust my decisions.
- My self-talk is strictly positive.
- I know which responsibilities are mine and which are not.
- I balance my empathy for others with personal boundaries and self-care.
- I am whole.
- I am grateful for my ongoing personal development.
- I can, and I will.
- I heal more every day.
- I am in control of what I think and how I feel.
- I am in control of my triggers.
- I am loving, intelligent, and creative, and I make positive changes in my life.
- I am a survivor and healed warrior.
- Today I give myself the freedom to make an error and know that it does not affect my worth as a human being.
- I deserve good things in life.
- My relationships are respectful and peaceful.
- I release old habits and practice new ones.
- I am excitedly hopeful. Healing is possible.
- I am connected with my authentic self.
- I express myself confidently.
- I hear my intuition and inner wisdom, and I listen.
- I am well and worthy.
- Today I honor and cherish my inner child, who was blameless then and now.

- I know and trust my own mind.
- My boundaries are a form of self-love.
- I stand in my truth, and I am heard.
- Only I can determine my self-worth.
- I easily see a person's authentic self, and I embrace what they're showing me.
- I listen to my wise self.
- Now is the time to step into my power.
- I am loved, loving and lovable.
- I can do hard things.
- I am here, I am alive, I am grateful, I am ready.
- I like myself.
- I am and always have been worthy.
- I am and always have been good enough.
- I focus on what's happening right now.
- When I have a problem, I focus on solutions.
- People like me.
- I am naturally relaxed and confident
- I am safe and secure.
- I am emotionally and physically strong.
- My appearance demonstrates that I value myself.
- I feel good about spending money on products and services to care for my body and demonstrate that I value myself.
- I take time for myself to rest, relax, unplug or do something that I enjoy.
- I allow peace into my life.
- I use my voice to protect myself.

Chapter Fourteen
HEALING SHAME

- I effectively communicate my needs and desires.
- I make a positive difference in the world.
- I love who I am, and I love my potential.
- I accept that others love the best they can and may be limited in their ability to express love.
- I honor and respect myself.
- I face my problems with courage and trust.
- I allow myself to be childlike.
- I let go of control and allow life to unfold.
- I ask for what I want.
- I clearly state my expectations.
- I dare to be imperfect.
- My voice empowers me.
- Today I create the life I want.
- I am centered and focused.
- I am capable and can easily handle anything that comes my way.
- I am unaffected by the desires of others.
- I embrace my inner child.
- I trust my inner voice.
- I let go of those not headed where I am going as a form of self-respect.
- I am unaffected by other's judgments.
- I repair relationships only with those willing to take their share of responsibility for what went wrong.
- Other's words have no power over me.
- Every decision I make is right for me.
- All is well in my life.

- I no longer live within the limitations of another's insecurity.
- I allow others the dignity of making their own choices.
- I let go of everything that does not promote positivity in my life.
- I am nourished and supported by my higher power.
- I am content with and enjoy my life
- I am connected to the infinite ancient wisdom of the universe, which guides me.
- I want for nothing; I have everything I need.
- I allow what I need to come to me.
- I let go and move on quickly and easily.
- I trust my higher power to nourish and support me.
- I easily let go of the need to understand everyone and everything.
- I let go of the need for others to understand me.
- I choose to trust and be open to all possibilities.
- I have confidence in myself.
- I am ready for everything that life offers me.
- I easily allow others their own journey.
- I am grounded and centered.
- I easily cultivate a group of like-minded people.
- I gain confidence with every action I take; I have everything I need to be successful.
- I embrace change. I am the author of my story.
- I am safe and secure at all times.
- Everything is working for my highest good.
- I am safe and protected in every situation.

- My emotions, mind, and spirit are all entirely safe and protected, now and always.
- I belong. I know that I am safe.
- I have everything I need. I am safe. I am loved.
- I feel safe wherever I am.
- I give my time and energy to those who deserve it.
- I allow the negative comments or behaviors of others to bounce off me.
- I release the negativity of toxic people.

My Healing Affirmations

- _____
- _____
- _____
- _____
- _____
- _____
- _____
- _____
- _____
- _____
- _____
- _____
- _____
- _____
- _____
- _____
- _____
- _____

Chapter Fifteen
EMOTIONALLY DETACHING

The term "narcissistic supply" defines the emotional feedback that narcissists need to keep their self-esteem intact. They get it from people in their environment. It's their "emotional food"; any form of attention or response will suffice.

A narcissistic mother feels a sense of power and importance from emotional reactions from others, especially her children. Any emotion—fear, sadness, anger, shame, whatever—will do because it feeds her false-self, making it stronger.

Like any narcissist, a narcissistic mom cannot survive without narcissistic supply.

NARCISSISTIC SUPPLY

Securing ongoing supply keeps a narcissist's false-self working in an automatic cycle: project the false-self, receive the supply, empower and strengthen the false-self, repeat.

The cycle repeats because it provides feelings of power, control, and importance. Narcissists, including narcissistic mothers, thrive on these feelings, which can make them feel formidable or even omnipotent after receiving supply, depending on the type and amount. This empowerment leads to a "narcissistic high," which can potentially be dangerous. You won't be permitted to share thoughts or feelings when your narcissist mom is on a high. She won't take challenges lightly and will go for the jugular to prove her supremacy. She's not interested in what you have to say or how you feel. When she's on a high, it's all about her.

Remember, narcissists don't view people as unique individuals with their own needs, feelings, goals, or lives. To narcissists, people are simply props who play a supporting role in *their* lives. A narcissist's only concerns are what they can get from others or what others can do for them. This makes it difficult for them to emotionally bond with others because relationships are all about power, control, and the benefits obtained.

Denying the Supply

When you are emotionally detached from your mother, you accept that she is entitled to make her own choices and deal with the consequences, all without your help! When you know how to use "loving" detachment, you can take your focus off of her and put it back on yourself and your life, where it belongs. And you *feel at peace* about whatever happens next.

This type of detachment (versus angry, apathetic, or numbing detachment styles) is judgment-free. It allows us to intellectually and emotionally separate from our mothers' hurtful behavior, not to punish or control, but as a demonstration of our own self-care.

Emotionally detaching is a great way to stop being a source of narcissistic supply. So is setting boundaries.

Another successful method to deny the supply is using the Gray Rock technique. This practice completely removes all emotional charge and drama from your interactions. When you use Gray Rock, **it removes all narcissistic supply.**

Say the following affirmations to remind you to focus on your life and maintain healthy limits.

AFFIRMATIONS TO SET AND MAINTAIN HEALTHY BOUNDARIES

- I deserve all the love, respect, joy, and prosperity that comes to me.
- I am compassionate and empathetic.
- I treat myself with honor and respect.
- I value myself.
- I am human. It's OK to be imperfect.
- I reaffirm for myself that I am on the right path.
- I embrace my new life even when it makes others uncomfortable.
- I acknowledge and protect my personal power.
- Today I take care of myself.
- I listen to my wise higher self.
- I allow others the freedom and dignity to learn from their mistakes.
- My boundaries are a form of self-love.
- This is stressful, so I take extra good care of myself today.
- I am a loveable person who deserves the care, affection, and respect of others.
- I make healthy choices for myself.
- I am kind and gentle with myself.
- It's OK for me to be afraid and courageous at the same time.
- I am doing the best that I can, and that's all I ask of myself.

- I ask for help when I am struggling.
- I have easy, mutually accepting relationships.
- I allow others to live their lives and release the need to worry or control.
- I am stronger than I thought.
- I value myself.
- I rely on my higher power for strength and guidance.
- I easily dial-up my confidence anytime I want.
- I am resilient.
- I am unaffected by other's negativity.
- I see the good things in myself.
- When I feel overwhelmed, I choose healthy ways to cope.
- I am intelligent and use my mind to make my life better.
- I have strong intuition, and I trust it even if I don't like what it tells me.
- When I see red flags occurring in people or relationships, I pay attention to them and respond accordingly.
- I ask for clarification when I am confused.
- I attract kind and caring people.
- I trust my decisions.
- My self-talk is strictly positive.
- I trust my senses of sight, hearing, smell, taste, and touch.
- I know which responsibilities are mine and which are not.

- I balance my empathy for others with personal boundaries and self-care.
- I am in control of my thoughts and actions.
- I am loving, intelligent, and creative and I make positive changes in my life.
- I am a survivor and healed warrior.
- Today I give myself the freedom to make an error and know that it does not affect my worth as a human being.
- I deserve good things in life.
- My relationships are respectful and peaceful.
- I release old habits and practice new ones.
- I am connected with my authentic self.
- I express myself confidently.
- I hear my intuition and inner wisdom, and I listen.
- I am well and worthy.
- I let go of controlling or manipulating others.
- I know and trust my own mind.
- I stand in my truth, and I am heard.
- Only I can determine my self-worth.
- I easily see a person's authentic self, and I embrace what they're showing me.
- I speak highly about _____, and they speak highly of me.
- Now is the time to step into my power.
- I am loved, loving and lovable.
- I can do hard things.
- I am and always have been worthy.
- I am and always have been good enough.

- I focus on what's happening right now.
- I let go of responsibilities that are not mine.
- I am smart and capable.
- When I have a problem, I focus on solutions.
- I am safe and secure.
- My body language demonstrates that I am sure of myself.
- I feel good about spending money on products and services to care for my body and demonstrate that I value myself.
- I take time for myself to rest, relax, unplug or do something that I enjoy.
- I allow peace into my life.
- I use my voice to protect myself.
- I attract joy into my life.
- I effectively communicate my needs and desires.
- I make a positive difference in the world.
- I accept that others love the best they can and may be limited in their ability to express love.
- I honor and respect myself.
- I face my problems with courage and trust.
- I ask for what I want.
- I clearly state my expectations.
- My voice empowers me.
- Today I create the life I want.
- I am centered and focused.
- I am capable and can easily handle anything that comes my way.
- I am unaffected by the desires of others.

- I trust my inner voice.
- I let go of those not headed where I am going as a form of self-respect.
- I am unaffected by other's judgments.
- I repair relationships only with those willing to take their share of responsibility for what went wrong.
- Other's words have no power over me.
- Every decision I make is right for me.
- I no longer live within the limitations of another's insecurity.
- I allow others the dignity of making their own choices.
- I let go of everything that does not promote positivity in my life.
- I am nourished and supported by my higher power.
- I cultivate inner peacefulness and gratitude.
- I allow what I need to come to me.
- I let go and move on quickly and easily.
- I easily let go of the need to understand everyone and everything.
- I let go of the need for others to understand me.
- I have confidence in myself.
- I easily allow others their own journey.
- I am grounded and centered.
- I acknowledge my pain, and I release it willingly and easily.
- I acknowledge my anger and release it willingly and easily.

- I gain confidence with every action I take; I have everything I need to be successful.
- I embrace change. I am the author of my story.
- Everything is working for my highest good.
- I am safe and protected in every situation.
- I give my time and energy to those who deserve it.
- I release the negativity of toxic people.
- I am happy and positive no matter who I am around.
- I let go of those who don't support and care about me.
- I know who deserves an explanation, who deserves an answer, and who deserves no response at all.

My Healing Affirmations

-
-
-
-
-
-
-
-
-
-
-
-
-
-
-
-
-
-
-
-

Chapter Sixteen
OVERCOMING THREATS AND RAGES

UNCONTROLLED OUTRAGE

Because narcissists are opinionated, argumentative, and defensive, they have no problem confronting, criticizing, or mocking anyone who challenges or disagrees with them.

Narcissists don't tolerate differences of opinion or perspectives. Instead, they gaslight, humiliate, insult, discredit, or have meltdowns known as narcissistic rages. Narcissistic rages are described as unexpected, uncontrolled angry outbursts. They are triggered by "narcissistic injuries," which are anything perceived as a threat to the "false-self."

Narcissistic rages look like adult "temper tantrums," except they're not cute, and they can be dangerous for those in the vicinity. When they're caught up in an angry outburst, narcissists are unreasonable and vengeful. Their objective is revenge. They want to win the argument and punish the offender, even if it means losing a relationship or irrevocably damaging one. As a result, they won't feel regret, remorse, or any need to apologize for their explosive, hurtful, or attention-seeking eruption.

Often, narcissistic rages are unwarranted. They are fear-based and sometimes persist even *after* the perceived threat is gone. Narcissistic moms can hang onto the memory of a transgression for weeks, months, or years at a time and use it as a justifiable reason for a rage. Narcissists are champion grudge holders because holding grudges vindicates their behavior and gives them a reason to feel victimized. Narcissist moms will bring up our wrongdoings as frequently as possible, playing "poor me" to receive sympathy and supply.

Sometimes rages don't actually look *angry*. Other kinds of rages are passive-aggressive. They involve sulking, giving backhanded compliments, procrastinating, making sarcastic remarks, withdrawing, sabotaging, undermining, or giving the silent treatment. Even though these methods are subtle and discreet, they're narcissistic rages nonetheless.

Please understand that your mother's narcissistic rages have nothing to do with you. You didn't cause her illness, you can't control it, and you can't cure it. But, you *can* control how you respond.

After witnessing a rage, use the following affirmations to start feeling secure again.

Affirmations to Feel Secure

- I love myself unconditionally.
- I use my voice, and I am heard.
- I listen when my heart talks to me.
- I acknowledge and protect my personal power.
- I am safe and free.
- I listen to my wise higher self.
- My boundaries are a form of self-love.
- I focus on what I can control, and I release the rest.
- This is stressful, so I take extra good care of myself today.
- I am a loveable person who deserves the care, affection, and respect of others.
- I make healthy choices for myself.
- I stay in the present and focus on one day at a time.
- I am kind and gentle with myself.
- I am getting through this by making healthy choices.
- I do everything I can to be physically and emotionally healthy.
- It's OK for me to be afraid and courageous at the same time.
- I am doing the best that I can, and that's all I ask of myself.
- I have easy, mutually accepting relationships.
- I am stronger than I thought.
- I lean on others for support, and I am lovingly supported.

- I value myself.
- I easily dial-up my confidence anytime I want.
- I acknowledge the things that I like about myself and add to that list regularly.
- I am resilient.
- I am unaffected by other's negativity.
- I see the good things in myself.
- When I feel overwhelmed, I choose healthy ways to cope.
- I am kind and empathetic.
- I am intelligent and use my mind to make my life better.
- I am a caring person, and people care about me.
- I have strong intuition, and I trust it even if I don't like what it tells me.
- When I see red flags occurring in people or relationships, I pay attention to them and respond accordingly.
- I trust my decisions.
- My self-talk is strictly positive.
- I trust my senses of sight, hearing, smell, taste, and touch.
- I know which responsibilities are mine and which are not.
- I balance my empathy for others with personal boundaries and self-care.
- I am whole.
- I am in control of my triggers.

- I am loving, intelligent, and creative, and I make positive changes in my life.
- I am a survivor and healed warrior.
- My relationships are respectful and peaceful.
- I release old habits and practice new ones.
- I am connected with my authentic self.
- I express myself confidently.
- I hear my intuition and inner wisdom, and I listen.
- I am well and worthy.
- I know and trust my own mind.
- Only I can determine my self-worth.
- I easily see a person's authentic self, and I embrace what they're showing me.
- Now is the time to step into my power.
- I am loved, loving and lovable.
- I can do hard things.
- I am here, I am alive, I am grateful, I am ready.
- I like myself.
- I am and always have been worthy.
- I am and always have been good enough.
- I focus on what's happening right now.
- I let go of responsibilities that are not mine.
- I am smart and capable.
- When I have a problem, I focus on solutions.
- People like me.
- I am naturally relaxed and confident.
- I am safe and secure.
- I am emotionally and physically strong.

- My body language demonstrates that I am sure of myself.
- My appearance demonstrates that I value myself.
- I take time for myself to rest, relax, unplug or do something that I enjoy.
- I allow peace into my life.
- I use my voice to protect myself.
- I attract joy into my life.
- I effectively communicate my needs and desires.
- I love who I am, and I love my potential.
- I release my wounds to my higher power.
- I accept that others love the best they can and may be limited in their ability to express love.
- I honor and respect myself.
- I allow myself to be childlike.
- I let go of control and allow life to unfold.
- I ask for what I want.
- I clearly state my expectations.
- I dare to be imperfect.
- My voice empowers me.
- Today I create the life I want.
- I am centered and focused.
- I am capable and can easily handle anything that comes my way.
- I am unaffected by the desires of others.
- I embrace my inner child.
- I trust my inner voice.

- I let go of those not headed where I am going as a form of self-respect.
- I am unaffected by other's judgments.
- I repair relationships only with those willing to take their share of responsibility for what went wrong.
- Other's words have no power over me.
- Every decision I make is right for me.
- All is well in my life.
- I no longer live within the limitations of another's insecurity.
- I let go of everything that does not promote positivity in my life.
- I am nourished and supported by my higher power.
- I am content with and enjoy my life.
- I cultivate inner peacefulness and gratitude.
- I am connected to the infinite ancient wisdom of the universe, which guides me.
- I let go and move on quickly and easily.
- I trust my higher power to nourish and support me.
- I easily let go of the need to understand everyone and everything.
- I let go of the need for others to understand me.
- I have confidence in myself.
- I easily allow others their own journey.
- I am grounded and centered.
- I easily cultivate a group of like-minded people.
- I acknowledge my pain, and I release it willingly and easily.

- I acknowledge my anger and release it willingly and easily.
- I gain confidence with every action I take; I have everything I need to be successful.
- I embrace change. I am the author of my story.
- I am safe and secure at all times.
- Everything is working for my highest good.
- I am safe and protected in every situation.
- I feel safe wherever I am.
- I give my time and energy to those who deserve it.
- I allow the negative comments or behaviors of others to bounce off me.
- I release the negativity of toxic people.
- I am happy and positive no matter who I am around.

My Healing Affirmations

- _____
- _____
- _____
- _____
- _____
- _____
- _____
- _____
- _____
- _____
- _____
- _____
- _____
- _____
- _____
- _____
- _____
- _____

Chapter Seventeen
HEALING FROM GASLIGHTING

SEEDS OF DOUBT

"Gaslighting" is a term borrowed from the 1938 stage play *Gaslight*. In this tale, a husband attempts to drive his wife insane by dimming their home's gas-powered lights and then denying it when his wife notices. This ploy causes her to doubt her perception, judgment, memory, and reality. As a result, she begins to believe she's losing her mind.

Narcissist moms intentionally gaslight their kids. Gaslighting is a form of emotional abuse. It is a mind game used to control beliefs, feelings, thoughts, perceptions, and actions. When we experience gaslighting, we react with cognitive dissonance, the mental anguish experienced from holding on to contradictory beliefs, ideas, or values. Our resulting confusion and turmoil provide our narcissistic mothers with instant and ongoing narcissistic supply.

A narcissist mom typically remains calm and rational after gaslighting her child, which, by contrast, makes the child feel insecure and irrational. You don't know what's happening when you're being gaslighted, but you intuitively know that your mother is intentionally doing it. You're primarily confused, stressed, and frustrated, and you can't figure out the reason. (Atkinson, Angela 2015).

Self-gaslighting

Self-gaslighting also contributes to cognitive dissonance.

When you try to convince yourself that you didn't just hear what you know you heard or that you didn't just see what you know you saw….you are self-gaslighting.

Do you gaslight yourself? I use the term "self-gaslighting" to describe the activity of minimizing or invalidating your mother's or anyone's hurtful behavior. For example, you're self-gaslighting when you make excuses for the behavior or convince yourself that it never happened (or that it didn't happen the way you remember it.) If you rewrite past events and persuade yourself to believe them, you're self-gaslighting.

When we self-gaslight, we tell ourselves that our mother's choice or behavior was our fault. We convince ourselves that we somehow provoked her hurtful behavior, or we take responsibility for the choices she made and the things she did that hurt us. We not only *accept* blame, but we intentionally place it on ourselves.

Gaslighting can have severe consequences. Whether by ourselves or someone else, when we're gaslighted regularly, the more doubtful and out-of-touch we feel We're unsure of what's real and what's not, what's true and what's not, and we don't know whether to believe our senses or only accept what we're *told*. If you're being gaslighted, you might begin lying or hiding to avoid stress or prevent your mother from becoming triggered, angry, or abusive. You'll also try to control outcomes because it offers a sense of predictability and stability.

Humans have a natural need for their attitudes, beliefs, and behaviors to exist amicably with each other. For those of us who've experienced gaslighting, it reduces us to confused, uncertain, dependent shadows of our former selves. It robs us of our ability to think, make decisions, and use sound judgment. We wind up doubting ourselves and fear that we're losing our minds. As targets of gaslighting, we may become so confused that we stop trusting our intuition and senses. Doing this gives a narcissistic mother considerable advantages (Newman, S. 2018).

We need to begin trusting our minds, senses, and memories again. Say the following affirmations to get started.

AFFIRMATIONS FOR IMPROVING SELF-TRUST

- I am compassionate and empathetic.
- I accept that pain is a part of my growth and personal development.
- I am grateful for all of the love that is in my life.
- I love myself unconditionally.
- I accept that others love the best way they know how.
- I let go of the need for others to validate me.
- I am human. It's OK to be imperfect.
- I listen when my heart talks to me.
- I know and trust my own mind.
- I love myself unconditionally.
- I accept that others love the best way they know how.
- I reaffirm for myself that I am on the right path.
- I embrace my new life even when it makes others uncomfortable.
- The past is over. I happily focus on the present moment, feeling empowered.
- I hear, affirm, comfort, and validate my inner child.
- I listen to my wise higher self.
- I am compassionate and empathetic.
- I allow others the freedom and dignity to learn from their mistakes.
- My boundaries are a form of self-love.
- This is stressful, so I take extra good care of myself today.
- I make healthy choices for myself.

- I stay in the present and focus on one day at a time.
- My body and mind need rest to recharge, so I let myself rest without judgment.
- I am kind and gentle with myself.
- I do everything I can to be physically and emotionally healthy.
- I am optimistic.
- It's OK for me to be afraid and courageous at the same time.
- I am doing the best that I can, and that's all I ask of myself.
- I ask for help when I am struggling.
- I allow others to live their lives and release the need to worry or control.
- I take work breaks to rest or have fun.
- I am stronger than I thought.
- I lean on others for support, and I am lovingly supported.
- I find something for which to be grateful every day.
- I value myself.
- I rely on my higher power for strength and guidance.
- I easily dial-up my confidence anytime I want.
- I acknowledge the things that I like about myself and add to that list regularly.
- I am resilient.
- I am unaffected by other's negativity.
- I see the good things in myself.
- I am kind and empathetic.

- I am intelligent and use my mind to make my life better.
- I am a caring person, and people care about me.
- I am compassionate and show my compassion in a variety of ways.
- I have strong intuition, and I trust it even if I don't like what it tells me.
- When I see red flags occurring in people or relationships, I pay attention to them and respond accordingly.
- I ask for clarification when I am confused.
- I attract mentally and emotionally stable people.
- I attract kind and caring people.
- My life gets better every day.
- When I slip up, I forgive myself and get back on track immediately.
- I trust my mind.
- I trust my decisions.
- My self-talk is strictly positive.
- I trust my senses of sight, hearing, smell, taste, and touch.
- I know which responsibilities are mine and which are not.
- I balance my empathy for others with personal boundaries and self-care.
- I am whole.
- I am grateful for my ongoing personal development.
- I can, and I will.
- I am in control of what I think and how I feel.

- I am in control of my triggers.
- I am loving, intelligent, and creative, and I make positive changes in my life.
- I am a survivor and healed warrior.
- Today I give myself the freedom to make an error and know that it does not affect my worth as a human being.
- I release old habits and practice new ones.
- I am excitedly hopeful. Healing is possible.
- I am connected with my authentic self.
- I express myself confidently.
- I hear my intuition and inner wisdom, and I listen.
- I am well and worthy.
- Today I honor and cherish my inner child, who was blameless then and now.
- I let go of controlling or manipulating others.
- I know and trust my own mind.
- I stand in my truth, and I am heard.
- Only I can determine my self-worth.
- I easily see a person's authentic self, and I embrace what they're showing me.
- Now is the time to step into my power.
- I am loved, loving and lovable.
- I can do hard things.
- I am here, I am alive, I am grateful, I am ready.
- I like myself.
- I am and always have been worthy.
- I am and always have been good enough.

- I take pleasure in my personal development.
- I focus on what's happening right now.
- I let go of responsibilities that are not mine.
- I am smart and capable.
- When I have a problem, I focus on solutions.
- People like me.
- I am naturally relaxed and confident.
- I am safe and secure.
- I am emotionally and physically strong.
- When I enter a room, I am poised and self-confident.
- My body language demonstrates that I am sure of myself.
- My appearance demonstrates that I value myself.
- I feel good about spending money on products and services to care for my body and demonstrate that I value myself.
- I take time for myself to rest, relax, unplug or do something that I enjoy.
- I allow peace into my life.
- I use my voice to protect myself.
- I attract joy into my life.
- I effectively communicate my needs and desires.
- I accept that others love the best they can and may be limited in their ability to express love.
- I honor and respect myself.
- I face my problems with courage and trust.
- I allow myself to be childlike.
- I let go of control and allow life to unfold.

- I ask for what I want.
- I clearly state my expectations.
- I dare to be imperfect.
- My voice empowers me.
- Today I create the life I want.
- I am centered and focused.
- I am capable and can easily handle anything that comes my way.
- I am unaffected by the desires of others.
- I embrace my inner child.
- I trust my inner voice.
- I let go of those not headed where I am going as a form of self-respect.
- I am unaffected by other's judgments.
- I repair relationships only with those willing to take their share of responsibility for what went wrong.
- I no longer live within the limitations of another's insecurity.
- My body achieves what my mind believes.
- I allow others the dignity of making their own choices.
- I let go of everything that does not promote positivity in my life.
- I am nourished and supported by my higher power.
- I cultivate inner peacefulness and gratitude.
- I am connected to the infinite ancient wisdom of the universe, which guides me.
- I want for nothing; I have everything I need.

- I surrender to the plans my higher power has in store for me.
- I allow what I need to come to me.
- I let go and move on quickly and easily.
- I have confidence in myself.
- I am ready for everything that life offers me.
- I easily allow others their own journey.
- I am grounded and centered.
- I acknowledge my pain, and I release it willingly and easily.
- I acknowledge my anger and release it willingly and easily.
- I give my time and energy to those who deserve it.
- I allow the negative comments or behaviors of others to bounce off me.
- I am happy and positive no matter who I am around.

My Healing Affirmations

- _____
- _____
- _____
- _____
- _____
- _____
- _____
- _____
- _____
- _____
- _____
- _____
- _____
- _____
- _____
- _____
- _____
- _____

Chapter Eighteen
HEALING CODEPENDENCY

Suppose we grow up in an environment that lacks nurturing. In that case, we may eventually begin neglecting ourselves to focus on others, emotionally caretaking them, fixing their problems, and anticipating their needs. Now everyone has the potential to become our priority.

We may even regard this self-sacrificing behavior as a positive thing.

In "Codependency for Dummies," Dr. Charles Whitfield says that codependency is "a disease of a lost self." When we're codependent, we "cut off" pieces of ourselves bit by bit until we are someone else's idea of who we should be. When I was highly codependent, there were times I wondered if there was ever an authentic "me" to begin with; it was so long since I'd seen her. As an adult, I didn't know the things about myself that I knew about my mother and others in my life. This was the result of an other-directed, other-focused childhood.

How Codependency Develops

Codependency is a set of maladaptive coping skills. If we became codependent as children, we were probably caretakers for our mothers and possibly other adults and siblings. We were likely required to mature quickly and take responsibilities that were not age-appropriate. When it felt unsafe being around our mothers, we learned to tiptoe around her instability not to upset her. We monitored her moods and responded accordingly. We noticed behavioral patterns, and we became very good at predicting her behavior. We learned how to take the initiative in making her life easier or better so *we* could feel a sense of stability and safety. We became accustomed to doing things for her and others that they could do for themselves.

As codependents, if we disappoint anyone, it can cause us to feel guilt and shame. Yet, we continually look for someone to please. We make excuses for their poor behavior or mistreatment of us, minimizing the pain we feel. If we hold onto this mindset and behavior pattern, we attract dysfunctional people. Those who have experienced maternal narcissistic abuse may eventually find themselves in abusive, toxic, or less-than-satisfying adult relationships. The new toxic person's behavior and way of relating seem familiar. We know our role and what's expected of us within the relationship.

Setting boundaries, saying "no," and letting others learn their life lessons "the hard way" are a great start to healing your codependent need to fix and control. So is allowing yourself to acknowledge and fully feel your emotions every day and continuing to validate yourself.

Codependency keeps us from our authentic selves. Affirmations are the opposite of codependency. When we're in touch with our authentic selves, we have the answers. The healing is inside of us. We hold on to our power and stand in our truth.

If you're codependent, it's essential to recover. Unresolved codependency has the potential to attract mentally unhealthy people into your life. It advertises your low self-esteem, self-worth, self-confidence. It infers that you will tolerate manipulation, maltreatment, and maybe even physical abuse. So if you're codependent, please do the work to heal it. The following affirmations will get you started.

AFFIRMATIONS TO HEAL CODEPENDENCY

- I am outgoing and confident.
- I boldly voice my opinions.
- I stand up for myself.
- I accept that pain is a part of my growth and personal development.
- I use my voice, and I am heard.
- I let go of the need for others to validate me.
- I value myself.
- I am human. It's OK to be imperfect.
- I embrace my new life even when it makes others uncomfortable.
- The past is over. I happily focus on the present moment, feeling empowered.
- I am in charge. Today's thoughts create my future.
- I acknowledge and protect my personal power.
- I hear, affirm, comfort, and validate my inner child.
- I easily attract _____.
- I allow others the freedom and dignity to learn from their mistakes.
- I allow without judgment.
- My boundaries are a form of self-love.
- I focus on what I can control, and I release the rest.
- I am a loveable person who deserves the care, affection, and respect of others.
- I make healthy choices for myself.
- I stay in the present and focus on one day at a time.

- My body and mind need rest to recharge, so I let myself rest without judgment.
- I am kind and gentle with myself.
- I do everything I can to be physically and emotionally healthy.
- I am optimistic.
- It's OK for me to be afraid and courageous at the same time.
- I am doing the best that I can, and that's all I ask of myself.
- I ask for help when I am struggling.
- I have easy, mutually accepting relationships.
- I allow others to live their lives and release the need to worry or control.
- I take work breaks to rest or have fun.
- I lean on others for support, and I am lovingly supported.
- I find something for which to be grateful every day.
- I value myself.
- I rely on my higher power for strength and guidance.
- I easily dial-up my confidence anytime I want.
- I acknowledge the things that I like about myself and add to that list regularly.
- I am resilient.
- I am unaffected by other's negativity.
- When I feel overwhelmed, I choose healthy ways to cope.
- I am kind and empathetic.

- I am intelligent and use my mind to make my life better.
- I have strong intuition, and I trust it even if I don't like what it tells me.
- When I see red flags occurring in people or relationships, I pay attention to them and respond accordingly.
- I ask for clarification when I am confused.
- I attract mentally and emotionally stable people.
- I attract kind and caring people.
- My life gets better every day.
- When I slip up, I forgive myself and get back on track immediately.
- I trust my mind.
- I trust my decisions.
- My self-talk is strictly positive.
- I trust my senses of sight, hearing, smell, taste, and touch.
- I know which responsibilities are mine and which are not.
- I balance my empathy for others with personal boundaries and self-care.
- I am whole.
- I am grateful for my ongoing personal development.
- I can, and I will.
- I heal more every day.
- I am in control of my thoughts and actions.
- I am in control of my triggers.

- I see my relationships improve as I prioritize my self-care.
- I am loving, intelligent, and creative, and I make positive changes in my life.
- I am a survivor and healed warrior.
- Today I give myself the freedom to make an error and know that it does not affect my worth as a human being.
- I deserve good things in life.
- My relationships are respectful and peaceful.
- I release old habits and practice new ones.
- I am excitedly hopeful. Healing is possible.
- I am connected with my authentic self.
- I express myself confidently.
- I hear my intuition and inner wisdom, and I listen.
- I am well and worthy.
- I let go of controlling or manipulating others.
- I know and trust my own mind.
- I stand in my truth, and I am heard.
- Only I can determine my self-worth.
- I speak highly about _____, and they speak highly of me.
- Now is the time to step into my power.
- I am loved, loving and lovable.
- I can do hard things.
- I am here, I am alive, I am grateful, I am ready.
- I like myself.
- I am and always have been worthy.

- I am and always have been good enough.
- I take pleasure in my personal development.
- I focus on what's happening right now.
- I let go of responsibilities that are not mine.
- I am naturally relaxed and confident.
- I am safe and secure.
- I am emotionally and physically strong.
- I feel good about spending money on products and services to care for my body and demonstrate that I value myself.
- I take time for myself to rest, relax, unplug or do something that I enjoy.
- I allow peace into my life.
- I use my voice to protect myself.
- I attract joy into my life.
- I effectively communicate my needs and desires.
- I make a positive difference in the world.
- I love who I am, and I love my potential.
- I release my wounds to my higher power.
- I accept that others love the best they can and may be limited in their ability to express love.
- I let go of control and allow life to unfold.
- I ask for what I want.
- I clearly state my expectations.
- I dare to be imperfect.
- My voice empowers me.
- Today I create the life I want.
- I am centered and focused.

- I am unaffected by the desires of others.
- I embrace my inner child.
- I trust my inner voice.
- I let go of those not headed where I am going as a form of self-respect.
- I am unaffected by other's judgments.
- I repair relationships only with those willing to take their share of responsibility for what went wrong.
- I am connected to the infinite ancient wisdom of the universe, which guides me.
- I allow what I need to come to me.
- I let go and move on quickly and easily.
- I trust my higher power to nourish and support me.
- I easily let go of the need to understand everyone and everything.
- I let go of the need for others to understand me.
- I choose to trust and be open to all possibilities.
- I have confidence in myself.
- I am ready for everything that life offers me.
- I easily allow others their own journey.
- I am grounded and centered.
- I gain confidence with every action I take.
- I embrace change. I am the author of my story.
- I give my time and energy to those who deserve it.

My Healing Affirmations

-
-
-
-
-
-
-
-
-
-
-
-
-
-
-
-
-
-

Chapter Nineteen
HEALING PTSD and C-PTSD

Children who experience neglect or ongoing traumatic abuse are at risk of developing Complex Post Traumatic Stress Disorder, depression, self-harming behaviors, and anxiety. They're also at risk for conduct, attachment, eating, and substance use disorders.

When these children become adults, they'll be at risk for revictimization. They'll also have a higher risk of developing physical illnesses like diabetes, heart disease, and immunological disorders. In addition, research shows that women who've suffered childhood abuse-related PTSD may have physically altered brains, and their cognitive functioning may be impaired.

PTSD vs. C-PTSD

Post-traumatic stress disorder (PTSD) is related to a single traumatic event. Complex Post Traumatic stress disorder (C-PTSD) is often the result of ongoing trauma and abuse.

When we are afflicted with C-PTSD, our minds attempt to ensure our safety by alerting us to stored memories of similar feeling threats. We may decide to avoid these painful memories, numbing them by actively denying, disconnecting from, and rejecting them (Phillips 2015), and the trauma *remains unaddressed and unhealed.*

People who have C-PTSD experience feelings of shame, guilt, or responsibility for the abuse. They may have difficulty controlling emotions, experience loss of attention and focus (dissociation), and isolation from friends and family. They may suffer from relationship difficulties or destructive or risky behavior such as alcohol or drug abuse, suicidal thoughts, chronic inflammatory disorders, mental exhaustion, anxiety, and self-gaslighting.

Triggering

As we've seen, unhealed traumatic memories can become triggers, highly sensitive, reactive emotions activated by our environment or someone's behavior or words.

Triggers alert us to recurring unhealed wounds, dangers, or threats. When we become triggered, we automatically react without thought and often feel like we're losing control. When we're triggered, we may quietly emotionally withdraw, or we may react intensely and aggressively. Either way, it's because we're protecting ourselves from a perceived threat, whether it's a real threat or just feels like one.

When we live with unresolved C-PTSD, it becomes challenging to navigate our daily lives and relationships. Emotional triggers are wounds that need to heal. Use the following affirmational statements to begin healing your triggers.

AFFIRMATIONS TO HEAL C-PTSD TRIGGERS

- I have confidence in myself.
- I release past hurts into the universe.
- I am grateful for all of the love that is in my life.
- I accept that others love the best way they know how.
- I let go of the need for others to validate me.
- I listen when my heart talks to me.
- The past is over. I happily focus on the present moment, feeling empowered.
- I acknowledge and protect my personal power.
- I am safe and free.
- My boundaries are a form of self-love.
- This is stressful, so I take extra good care of myself today.
- I make healthy choices for myself.
- I stay in the present and focus on one day at a time.
- My body and mind need rest to recharge, so I let myself rest without judgment.
- I am kind and gentle with myself.
- I am getting through this by making healthy choices.
- I am optimistic.
- It's OK for me to be afraid and courageous at the same time.
- I am doing the best that I can, and that's all I ask of myself.
- I ask for help when I am struggling.

- I lean on others for support, and I am lovingly supported.
- I find something for which to be grateful every day.
- This feeling will pass.
- When I feel overwhelmed, I choose healthy ways to cope.
- I am intelligent and use my mind to make my life better.
- I have strong intuition, and I trust it even if I don't like what it tells me.
- When I see red flags occurring in people or relationships, I pay attention to them and respond accordingly.
- I ask for clarification when I am confused.
- I attract mentally and emotionally stable people.
- I attract kind and caring people.
- When I slip up, I forgive myself and get back on track immediately.
- I trust my mind.
- I trust my decisions.
- My self-talk is strictly positive.
- I trust my senses of sight, hearing, smell, taste, and touch.
- I know which responsibilities are mine and which are not.
- I balance my empathy for others with personal boundaries and self-care.
- I hear, affirm, comfort, and validate my inner child.
- I am whole.

- I am grateful for my ongoing personal development.
- I can, and I will.
- I heal more every day.
- I am in control of my thoughts and actions.
- I am in control of what I think and how I feel.
- I am in control of my triggers.
- I am loving, intelligent, and creative, and I make positive changes in my life.
- I am a survivor and healed warrior.
- I release old habits and practice new ones.
- I am excitedly hopeful. Healing is possible.
- I am connected with my authentic self.
- I express myself confidently.
- I hear my intuition and inner wisdom, and I listen.
- I am well and worthy.
- I know and trust my own mind.
- Only I can determine my self-worth.
- I easily see a person's authentic self, and I embrace what they're showing me.
- My words are kind and loving.
- Now is the time to step into my power.
- I am loved, loving and lovable.
- I can do hard things.
- I am here, I am alive, I am grateful, I am ready.
- I like myself.
- I am and always have been worthy.
- I am and always have been good enough.
- I focus on what's happening right now.

- I am smart and capable.
- People like me.
- I am naturally relaxed and confident.
- I am safe and secure.
- I am emotionally and physically strong.
- I take time for myself to rest, relax, unplug or do something that I enjoy.
- I allow peace into my life.
- I use my voice to protect myself.
- I effectively communicate my needs and desires.
- I make a positive difference in the world.
- I love who I am, and I love my potential.
- I release my wounds to my higher power.
- I accept that others love the best they can and may be limited in their ability to express love.
- I honor and respect myself.
- I face my problems with courage and trust.
- I allow myself to be childlike.
- I clearly state my expectations.
- My voice empowers me.
- I am centered and focused.
- I am capable and can easily handle anything that comes my way.
- I am unaffected by the desires of others.
- I embrace my inner child.
- I trust my inner voice.
- Other's words have no power over me.
- Every decision I make is right for me.

- All is well in my life.
- I no longer live within the limitations of another's insecurity.
- I allow others the dignity of making their own choices.
- I let go of everything that does not promote positivity in my life.
- I am nourished and supported by my higher power.
- I am content with and enjoy my life
- I cultivate inner peacefulness and gratitude.
- I am connected to the infinite ancient wisdom of the universe, which guides me.
- I want for nothing; I have everything I need.
- I surrender to the plans my higher power has in store for me.
- I allow what I need to come to me.
- I let go and move on quickly and easily.
- I easily let go of the need to understand everyone and everything.
- I let go of the need for others to understand me.
- I choose to trust and be open to all possibilities.
- I am ready for everything that life offers me.
- I easily allow others their own journey.
- I am grounded and centered.
- I acknowledge my pain, and I release it willingly and easily.
- I acknowledge my anger and release it willingly and easily.

- I am safe and secure at all times.
- Everything is working for my highest good.
- My emotions, mind, and spirit are all entirely safe and protected, now and always.
- I belong. I know that I am safe.
- I have everything I need. I am safe. I am loved.
- I feel safe wherever I am.
- I allow the negative comments or behaviors of others to bounce off me.
- I release the negativity of toxic people.
- I am happy and positive no matter who I am around.
- I let go of those who don't support and care about me.

My Healing Affirmations

- _____
- _____
- _____
- _____
- _____
- _____
- _____
- _____
- _____
- _____
- _____
- _____
- _____
- _____
- _____
- _____
- _____
- _____

Chapter Twenty
A NEW BEGINNING

Those of us who've been affected by maternal narcissism need to heal and reclaim our identity and emotional balance.

As we've seen, healing requires doing specific work to address particular trauma symptoms. To recover, most of us need to progress through the stages of Narcissism Awareness Grief, eliminate codependency, and set healthy boundaries. Doing these with the help of a trained therapist or support group will keep us on track and keep us from getting stuck.

Speaking affirmations is a healing work that can change your mindset, help you connect with your authentic self, and create the life you desire. Healing affirmations are a great tool to use along with the others in your healing-arsenal.

By learning to write your own powerful healing affirmations and integrating them into your daily routine, you can expedite your recovery. After using your healing affirmations for a few weeks, notice the changes in your thinking and perceiving. Notice how you feel emotionally. The order in which the changes occur is irrelevant. You'll start healing where and when you need to, on your own exclusive timetable. As you heal, you will finally be able to move forward to live beyond your fabricated childhood reality.

In "Lemon Moms: A Guide to Understand and Survive Maternal Narcissism," I listed several recovery indicators that I'm including here also.

Keep track of your progress, and add each new indicator to your gratitude list as you continue writing and using healing affirmations.

Indicators of Recovery

- You're beginning to respect yourself.

- You've set some new boundaries.

- You focus more on what makes you happy and what's important to you rather than making others happy or knowing what's important to them.

- You've found activities that you love, and you do them regularly.

- You're in touch with your intuition, and you're learning to trust it.

- You realize it's not your job, and it never was your job to treat or fix your mother or anyone else.

- You've examined your childhood programming and questioned each of the misperceptions you were expected to believe. You're working on letting go of your mother's faulty perceptions of you.

- You're creating new ideas about who you are, based on how far you've come and who you are today.

- When you see narcissistic behavior, you recognize it for what it is, and you steer clear.

- You're learning to fulfill your own needs, and you don't feel guilty about it.

- You recognize that your mother has a problem with thinking and perceiving and that she'll probably never address it.

- You understand that the crazy-making feelings you had around your mother were a normal reaction to her abnormal behavior. Your brain was functioning precisely the way it was supposed to, to protect and help you try to make sense of a situation that would never make sense.

- You're aware of when you're self-gaslighting, and you stop as soon as you become aware.
- You feel grounded and safe most of the time.
- You're getting comfortable having difficult conversations.
- You're getting comfortable confronting people who need to be confronted.
- You stand up for yourself calmly and confidently.
- You are fiercely on your own side.
- A person's character and integrity matter more to you than their popularity, sense of humor, success, or physical attributes.
- You're not interested in continuing people-pleasing behaviors.
- You like yourself much of the time.
- You're aware of your self-talk, and make sure that it's positive.
- You focus more often on what makes you happy and what is important to you.

- You're developing personal values.

- You're working through your anger.

- You're working on forgiveness.

- You're learning to allow others to earn your trust.

- You notice when "red flags" are present. Then, when it's not possible to avoid those individuals, you maintain low contact and enforce your boundaries.

- You're doing recovery work regularly and acknowledging your progress.

- You believe that you're a strong person.

- You're educating yourself about narcissism, toxic people, and toxic relationships.

- You're creating new beliefs about yourself based on who you've become and who you are becoming.

- You've begun to prioritize self-care in its many forms.

- You seek out and practice guided meditations that help you feel positive, strong, and peaceful.

- You journal.

- You no longer allow people or events to intrude on your plans, privacy, safety, or serenity.

- You don't worry about whether your life choices will make your mother angry or upset. You're making life choices that are all about *you* now.

- When a narcissist invites you to an argument, you decline.

- You're aware of relationships that take advantage of you.

- You focus on solutions, not problems.

- You're more concerned about your life than anyone else's.

- You no longer tolerate people who devalue or disrespect you. You kick them out of your life, and you feel good about doing it.

- You're becoming your own advocate.

- You're beginning to know what's good for you and what isn't.

- You're no longer willing to accept someone else's version of reality.

- You're not willing to minimize your education, talents, skills, or abilities to accommodate someone else's insecurities.

- You're not willing to minimize your education, talents, skills, or abilities to accommodate someone else's faulty perception of you.

- You know when you're being manipulated by guilt, shame, passive-aggressive behavior, and other forms of control, and you no longer let yourself be controlled.

- You're getting comfortable communicating about the things you will and won't accept or do in your relationships.

- You recognize when you're being gaslighted and refuse to let your reality be re-written by someone else.

- You'll absolutely leave situations that make you feel uncomfortable or unsafe.

- You feel worthy of being seen and heard.

- You're uncomfortable when you're in denial, and you recognize it for what it is.

- You recognize that you are a complete person, and you don't need validation or acceptance from anyone except yourself.

- You don't need permission to exist

- You're no longer interested in being a people-pleaser. You understand and accept that this kind of enabling behavior makes you a potential victim.

- You refuse to give up your own plans or dreams so someone else can achieve their own.

- You refuse to spend your precious time doing things you don't want to do that might gain someone's attention, affection, approval, or love.

- You've decided to stop over-functioning.

- You've decided to stop "rowing the boat" all by yourself. You understand and believe that others need to do their share of the work.

- You say "no" more often and set limits for other's behavior and expectations.

- You understand that there are consequences for every action, and you let others deal with theirs.

- You recognize that all relationships are two-way interactions.

- You no longer make excuses for or minimize someone else's behavior.

- You don't tolerate "walking on eggshells."

- You empathize, but you draw the line at being taken advantage of.

- You realize that boundaries work two ways: you no longer violate other's boundaries by rescuing or trying to fix them or their circumstances.

- You ask for clarification when you're confused by something someone says or does.

- You're getting comfortable disengaging from toxic people, and you know when and why it's necessary.

- You recognize that people who use mind-games, manipulation, secrecy, intimidation, hurtful sarcasm or teasing, are toxic individuals, and you enforce the boundaries that protect you.

- You see that praise, flattery, compliments, or charm can be subtle forms of manipulation, and those simply don't work on you anymore.

- You're not willing to stay in a relationship that makes you feel drained, confused, or doubtful of your sanity or self-worth.

- You don't tolerate others crossing your boundaries or talking about: your appearance, weight, relationships, or achievements.

- You accept yourself in all your imperfection.

- You understand that "perfection" doesn't exist and that your vulnerabilities, strengths, and weaknesses all combine to create the complete and lovable person you are.

- You trust your decision-making abilities, and you make decisions more easily.

Whether you're starting your healing journey or adding affirmations to your existing arsenal, I hope you do the work and keep moving forward. You can do hard things!

Here's to continued healing, lifelong self-improvement, and enjoying life as your authentic self! I wish you the best.

Glossary of Terms

Amygdala: an almond-shaped structure in the brain involved with experiencing emotions. There are two, one on each side of the brain.

Boundaries: protect us from someone else's behavior or engaging in activities that we'd rather not. Setting healthy boundaries protect and empower us regarding our safety, emotional stability, and mental health.

Codependent (enabler): an individual with an emotional and behavioral illness affecting their ability to have healthy, mutually satisfying relationships. Codependency is a learned behavior, so it's passed down through generations. It occurs when a person supports or enables another person's addiction, mental illness, immaturity, irresponsibility, or under-achievement. Codependents rely on others for a sense of identity, approval, or affirmation. They are "people-pleasers" who willingly play by the "rules" of others, losing their own identity in the process.

Cognitive dissonance: the mental discomfort experienced from holding two or more contradictory beliefs, ideas, or values.

Cognitive empathy: having the *intellectual* understanding that someone is feeling a particular emotion but not feeling anything in response to that awareness.

Complex-Post-traumatic Stress Disorder (C-PTSD): results from a series of trauma-causing events or one prolonged event, whereas PTSD is usually related to a single traumatic event. Complex-Post-traumatic Stress Disorder can be the result of narcissistic abuse. Common symptoms include flashbacks, panic attacks, nightmares, overactive startle response, habitually thinking about the traumatic event.

Dissociation: losing the sense of "who I am, where I am, or of what I'm doing." It's a protective response that allows emotional separation from trauma or abuse as it's happening.

Ego: the part of the mind that arbitrates between the conscious and the unconscious. It's responsible for our sense of self, personal identity, and the filter through which we see ourselves. We tell our egos specific "stories" to continue living with certain self-defining beliefs.

Emotional empathy: the ability to put ourselves in another person's place and feel the emotions they're feeling.

Enabling: taking responsibility, blame, or making excuses for a person's harmful or hurtful behavior. Also known as Codependency.

Gaslighting: a tactic used to gain power and control over an individual by prompting them to doubt their senses or memory. The goal of gaslighting is to cause someone to question their reality and doubt their memory and judgment.

Gray rock: a way of encouraging an emotionally unbalanced person to lose interest by training them to view you as uninteresting or boring.

Hippocampus: a brain structure located under the cerebral cortex and part of the limbic system. It plays a vital role in moving information from short-term to long-term memory.

Law of Attraction: thinking positive thoughts can bring about positive effects, and negative thoughts can bring negative outcomes. Based on the belief that thoughts are a form of energy, positive thoughts attract positive energy and vice versa.

Learned helplessness: a state in which a person feels a sense of powerlessness from experiencing a traumatic event or continual failure. It is believed sometimes to be an underlying cause of depression.

Loving detachment: means "caring enough about others to allow them to learn from their mistakes. It also means being responsible for our own welfare and making decisions without ulterior motives or the desire to control others." -Al-Anon literature

Mixed message: a type of communication where an individual gives conflicting information, either verbal or non-verbal.

Narcissism Awareness Grief: Much like the famous Kubler-Ross "five stages of grief," there are several stages of Narcissism Awareness Grief. They're not linear, so they're not experienced in any particular order. In fact, we can go back and forth between the stages throughout the process of grieving. But every step must be experienced to get to the final stage of "acceptance." It's possible to become stuck in any phase for any length of time and never actually enter into acceptance. The difference between the two grief models is that NAG has an additional and essential stage called "rewriting." (Hammond 2019). This is where profound healing begins.

Narcissistic injury: anything a narcissist perceives as a threat to their false self or their sense of importance and dominance.

Narcissistic Personality Disorder (NPD): a disorder recognized by the DSM, characterized by these nine criteria:

- grandiose sense of self-importance

- preoccupied with fantasies of unlimited success, power, beauty, etc.

- believes s/he is 'special' and can only be understood by or associate with like-minded people

- requires excessive admiration
- feels entitled to, and expects special treatment
- manipulative and exploitative
- lacks empathy
- envious of others or believes others are envious of them
- arrogant or haughty behavior.

To be diagnosed with narcissism, at least five of these specific traits must be expressed.

Narcissistic rage: intense anger, aggression, or passive-aggression displayed by a narcissist when they experience a setback or challenges their illusion of grandiosity, entitlement, or superiority, triggering their inadequacy, shame, or vulnerability. –Psychology Today, July 8, 2018

Narcissistic supply (NS): a concept introduced into psychoanalytic theory by Otto Fenichel in 1938, describing a type of admiration and support a narcissist takes from their environment. It is essential to their self-esteem.

No contact (NC): an example of a boundary used to prevent recurring abuse. It is usually considered to be a "last resort" for protection against dysfunctional or abusive behavior.

Passive-aggression: involves showing aggression in a passive, more socially acceptable way.

Projection: the attribution of a trait we dislike in ourselves onto someone else.

Quantum self: the subatomic realm of human consciousness.

Reaction: a reciprocal or counteracting force, typically quick, without much thought. Aggressive.

Response: a thoughtful, calm, and non-threatening reply.

Scapegoating: a practice seen in dysfunctional families. The scapegoat is the person who gets blamed for offenses and injustices that happen to family members, and the role can be temporary or permanent. Family members other than the narcissistic mom take turns in the scapegoat role. The mom determines the scapegoat.

Self-gaslighting: a form of self-doubt and self-deception that contributes to maintaining codependency. It's a consequence of accepting continual blame or living in a dysfunctional environment with inadequate emotional support.

Silent treatment: a way to inflict pain without causing visible marks. Research shows that "ignoring" or "excluding" someone activates the part of the brain where physical pain is experienced.

Trauma bond: powerful emotional bonds that are created between two individuals undergoing cycles of abuse together. Over time trauma bonds become very resistant to change, and a codependent relationship develops.

Triggering: reacting to old, buried memories with a knee-jerk, unconscious behavior. Triggers indicate unhealed wounds.

Validation: the act of recognizing or affirming someone's feelings or thoughts as sound or worthwhile. Validation is an essential aspect of mothering because it contributes to effective and safe communication. Feeling heard and understood leads to feelings of trust, a cornerstone of every relationship.

References

Aronson E. (1969). The theory of cognitive dissonance: a current perspective. In Berkowitz, L. (editor). *Advances in Experimental Social Psychology*. New York: Academic Press, 1–34.

Atkinson, Angela (2015). *Take back your life: 103 highly-effective strategies to snuff out a narcissist's gaslighting and enjoy the happy life you really deserve.*

Baskin-Sommers, A., Krusemark, E., & Ronningstam, E. (2014, July). *Empathy in Narcissistic Personality Disorder: from clinical and empirical perspectives.* Retrieved July 10, 2019, from https://www.ncbi.nlm.nih.gov/pmc/articles/PMC4415495/

Becker, R, Selden, G. (1985) The body electric: Electromagnetism and the Foundations of life. William Morrow Publ, N. Y.

Brenner, Grant Hilary. (2018, September 5) *"Is projection the most powerful defense mechanism?"* Psychology Today, Sussex Publishers. Retrieved August 12, 2019, from https://www.psychologytoday.com/us/blog/experimentations/201809/is-projection-the-most-powerful-defense-mechanism.

Burgo, Joseph. The narcissist you know: defending yourself against extreme narcissists in an all-about-me age. New York: Touchstone, 2016.

Cascio, C.N., Brook O'Donnell, M., Tinney, F.J., Lieberman, M.D., Taylor, S.E., Strecher, V.J., Falk, E.B. Self-affirmation activates brain systems associated with self-related processing and reward and is reinforced by future orientation, *Social Cognitive and Affective Neuroscience*, Volume 11, Issue 4, April 2016, Pages 621–629, https://doi. org/10.1093/scan/nsv136.

Cohen, G. L., & Sherman, D. K. (2007). Self-affirmation theory. In R. Baumeister and K. Vohs (Eds.), Encyclopedia of Social Psychology (pp. 787-789). Thousand Oakes: Sage Publications.

Cohen, G. L., & Sherman, D. K. (2014). The psychology of change: Self-affirmation and social psychological intervention. *Annual Review of Psychology, 65*, 333-371.

Cooke, R., Trebaczyk, H., Harris, P., & Wright, A.J. (2014) Self-affirmation promotes physical activity. *Journal of Sport and Exercise Psychology, 36*(2), 217–223.

Critcher, C. R., & Dunning, D. (2015). Self-affirmations provide a broader perspective on self-threat. *Personality and Social Psychology Bulletin*, 41(1), 3-18.

Eisenberger, N. I., Lieberman, M. D., & Williams, K. D. (2004). *Does rejection hurt? An fMRI study of social exclusion.* PsycEXTRA Dataset. doi: 10.1037/e633912013-635.

Epton, T., & Harris, P. R. (2008). Self-affirmation promotes health behavior change. *Health Psychology, 27*(6), 746–752. https://doi.org/10.1037/0278-6133.27.6.746

Falk, E. B., O'Donnell, M. B., Cascio, C. N., Tinney, F., Kang, Y., Lieberman, M. D., Taylor, S. E., An, L., Resnicow, K., & Strecher, V. J. (2015). Self-affirmation alters the brain's response to health messages and subsequent behavior change. *Proceedings of the National Academy of Sciences, 112*(7), 1977–1982. https://doi.org/10.1073/pnas.1500247112

Gerber, R. (2001) A Practical Guide to Vibrational Medicine: Energy Healing and Spiritual Transformation *HarperCollins, N. Y.*

Hammond, C. (2019, June 29). What is narcissism awareness grief (NAG)? Retrieved August 2, 2019, from https://pro.psychcentral.com/exhausted-woman/2018/07/what-is-narissism-awareness-grief-nag/

Harris, P. R., Mayle, K., Mabbott, L., & Napper, L. (2007). Self-affirmation reduces smokers' defensiveness to graphic on-pack cigarette warning labels. *Health Psychology, 26,* 437–446.

Keyes, Corey & Fredrickson, Barbara & Park, Nansook & Keyes, Corey. (2012). Positive Psychology and the Quality of Life. 10.1007/978-94-007-2421-1_5.

Koole, S. L., Smeets, K., van Knippenberg, A., & Dijksterhuis, A. (1999). The cessation of rumination through self-affirmation. Journal of Personality and Social Psychology, 77(1), 111–125. https://doi.org/10.1037/0022-3514.77.1.111

Layous, K., Davis, E. M., Garcia, J., Purdie-Vaughns, V., Cook, J. E., & Cohen, G. L. (2017). Feeling left out, but affirmed: Protecting against the negative effects of low belonging in college. *Journal of Experimental Social Psychology, 69*, 227-231.

Logel, C., & Cohen, G.L. (2012). The role of the self in physical health: Testing the effect of a values-affirmation intervention on weight loss. *Psychological Science, 23*(1), 53–55

McQueen, A., & Klein, W. M. (2006). Experimental manipulations of self-affirmation: A systematic review. Self and Identity, 5(4), 289-354

Newman, S. (2018, July 8). *3 Reasons you can't win with a narcissist.* Retrieved September 12, 2019, from https://psychcentral.com/blog/3-reasons-you-cant-win-with-a-narcissist/

Phillips, J. (2015, September 25). PTSD in DSM-5: Understanding the changes. Retrieved August 30, 2019, from https://www.psychiatrictimes.com/ptsd/ptsd-dsm-5-understanding-changes.

Pune Mirror | Updated: Jul 2, 2019. (n.d.). *Is the 'silent treatment' killing your relationship?* Retrieved November 17, 2019, from https://punemirror.indiatimes.com/others/you/is-the-silent-treatment-killing-your-relationship/articleshow/70029879.cms.

Saeed, K. (2019, August 5). *How to deal with the silent treatment and gain the upper hand.* Retrieved December 22, 2019, https://kimsaeed.com/2019/07/28/how-to-deal-with-the-silent-treatment-and-gain-the-upper-hand/.

Sherman, D. K., & Cohen, G. L. (006). The psychology of self-defense: Self-affirmation theory. In M. P. Zanna (Ed.) Advances in experimental social psychology, 38, pp. 183-242. New York, NY: Guildford Press.

Sherman, D. K., Cohen, G. L., Nelson, L. D., Nussbaum, A. D., Bunyan, D. P., & Garcia, J. (2009). Affirmed yet unaware: Exploring the role of awareness in the process of self-affirmation. *Journal of Personality and Social Psychology, 97*, 745-764.

Steele, C. M. (1988). The psychology of self-affirmation: Sustaining the integrity of the self. Advances in experimental social psychology, 21, 261-302

Wiesenfeld, B. M., Brockner, J., Petzall, B., Wolf, R., & Bailey, J. (2001). Stress and coping among layoff survivors: A self-affirmation analysis. Anxiety, Stress & Coping: An International Journal, 14(1), 15–34. https://doi.org/10.1080/10615800108248346

Bibliography

3 Steps to identifying a narcissist. (n.d.). Retrieved from https://www.psychologytoday.com/us/blog/5-types-people-who-can-ruin-your-life/201808/3-steps-identifying-narcissist.

Dodgson, L. (2018, May 27). *How to spot a covert narcissist.* Retrieved July 19, 2019, from https://www.businessinsider.com/how-to-spot-a-covert-narcissist-2018-5.

Ford, J. D. (2005). Treatment implications of altered affect regulation and information processing following child maltreatment. *Psychiatric Annals*, 35(5), 410-419. doi:10.3928/00485713-20050501-07.

Peterson, S. (2018, June 11). *Effects.* Retrieved Jan 24, 2019, from https://www.nctsn.org/what-is-child-trauma/trauma-types/complex-trauma/effects.

Schneider, A. (2015, March 25). *Idealize, devalue, discard: the dizzying cycle of narcissism.* Retrieved July 23, 2019, from https://www.goodtherapy.org/blog/idealize-devalue-discard-the-dizzying-cycle-of-narcissism-0325154.

Srinivasan T. (2010). Energy medicine. *International journal of yoga*, 3(1), 1. https://doi.org/10.4103/0973-6131.66770

Streep, P. (2017). *How narcissistic parents scapegoat their children.* Retrieved July 26, 2019, from https://www.psychologytoday.com/us/blog/tech-support/201711/how-narcissistic-parents-scapegoat-their-children.

Tips, R., & Children, P. (2019). *Psychologists confirm narcissistic parents are incapable of loving their children.* Retrieved Jan 24, 2019, from https://iheartintelligence.com/narcissistic-parents-incapable-of-loving-their-children/.

Toll, A. (2013). *Be honest with me: an exploration of lies in relationships.* Retrieved Jan 10, 2019, from https://dc.uwm.edu/cgi/viewcontent.cgi?article=1168&context=etd.

Enhance Your Experience

Learn strategies to heal childhood trauma caused by mothers who are unable to properly bond with their children-

Subscribe to:

The **Toolbox**:

toolbox.dianemetcalf.com

Support, Validation, and Healing

Receive new content twice per month.

The Toolbox is the place to learn healthy coping skills, challenge your thinking, and take back your personal power. It's where you can begin recovering from the effects of toxic people and unhealthy relationships, especially narcissistic mothers.

Acknowledgments

I wish to thank those whose efforts and encouragement have helped me bring yet another edition into The Lemon Moms Series; Support, Validation, and Healing. It has indeed become a legacy of recovery.

In 2020, that unforgettable year of the Corona Virus pandemic and worldwide lockdowns, I was unexpectedly gifted with extra time and solitude. Although the isolation and confinement took their respective tolls, I am grateful for the learning opportunities they provided. I was allowed the privilege of working with Intuitive Life Coach Ellen Maree and, through her, discovering more about the fabulous tool of self-affirmation. Thank you, my new friend!

Thank you to my proofreaders, Christin D'Aurelio, Susan Brooks, Val Catallozzi, and Gayle Shinder, for sharing your perspectives and honest feedback. I love and appreciate each of you. Your feedback, corrections, advice, and suggestions made the difference!

To my immediate family; daughter Christin, son, Matt, and husband, Kim: I love, respect, and appreciate each of you more than you'll ever know. You make my world a shiny, happy place.

About the Author

Diane Metcalf is an experienced advocate, speaker, and writer on domestic violence, abuse, and family dysfunction. She holds a Bachelor of Arts degree in Psychology and a Master of Science in Information Technology.

She has held social worker, counselor, and program manager positions in domestic violence and abuse, senior healthcare, developmental disabilities, and reproductive health. She is an experienced advocate and speaker on the topics of domestic violence and abuse. She has experienced maternal narcissistic abuse, developed coping skills and strategies, and shares those insights with those who want to heal.

This book is a compilation resulting from her education, knowledge, and personal insight regarding her own traumatic experiences and subsequent recovery work. She is no longer a practicing social worker, counselor, program manager, or advocate.

Diane lives in Las Vegas, Nevada, with her husband Kim and her goofy, adorable Goldador, Abby, and her lovable, affectionate tabby, Simba. She continues to write about toxic relationships and recovery on her blog, The Toolbox (toolbox.dianemetcalf.com.)

This book is intended for informational purposes only and is not a substitute for professional therapy.

What's Next?

Heal Your Narcissism Victim Syndrome:

1. *Lemon Moms: A Guide to Understand and Survive Maternal Narcissism*

2. *The Lemon Moms Companion Workbook: Action Steps to Understand and Survive Maternal Narcissism*

3. *Lemon Moms Life-Altering Affirmations: Change Your Self-talk, Change YourSELF*

All available on Amazon.com and wherever books are sold!

Author's WebSite:

DianeMetcalf.com

Love This Book?

Don't forget to leave a review!

Every review matters!

Your review will help others determine whether this book is helpful.

Head over to wherever you purchased this book and let other readers know your thoughts.

Thank you so much. I appreciate you!

www.ingramcontent.com/pod-product-compliance
Lightning Source LLC
Chambersburg PA
CBHW071234070526
44583CB00017B/2184